Voices of Experience

How Teachers Manage Student-Centered ESL Classes

Janet Giannotti
NORTHERN VIRGINIA COMMUNITY COLLEGE

ANN ARBOR
UNIVERSITY OF MICHIGAN PRESS

Copyright © by University of Michigan 2015
All rights reserved
Published in the United States of America
The University of Michigan Press
Manufactured in the United States of America

∞ Printed on acid-free paper

ISBN-13: 978-0-472-03614-1

2018 2017 2016 2015   4 3 2 1

No part of this publication may be reproduced, stored in a retrieval system, or transmitted in any form or by any means, electronic, mechanical, or otherwise, without the written permission of the publisher.

Preface

When the theme for TESOL 2012 in Philadelphia was announced as "A Declaration of Excellence," I was inspired by the Declaration of Independence to propose a session titled "Are These Classroom Management Truths Self-Evident?" To my delight, this session was accepted. In my proposal, I wrote:

> While the Declaration of Independence claims that some truths are held to be self-evident, can we say the same for the truths of classroom management? Is the truth about classroom management evident to novice teachers? What bits of wisdom can veteran teachers impart to new teachers? The presenter celebrates her 35th anniversary as a classroom teacher by sharing twenty truths about teaching adult ESL students. A lighthearted approach addresses many serious issues, from dealing with late arrivals to individualizing instruction, and from answering questions to eliminating cheating. The presentation offers new teachers a chance to learn some tricks and veteran teachers a chance to share their favorite techniques.

My presentation was well received, and overall I was struck by how the participants were eager to weigh in with their challenges and solutions.

Some of the twenty "truths" from my own presentation are listed here.

- ❏ Your students will arrive late.
- ❏ You will repeat answers and explanations that you already gave.
- ❏ Students can write on the board too.
- ❏ Your place in the room matters.
- ❏ If you sit down with a small group of students, they are more likely to talk to you.

- ❏ You can stop students from cheating on quizzes.
- ❏ Your students work at vastly different paces.
- ❏ You are not in control of the learning that takes place in your classroom.

As I mentioned, the participants in my TESOL session were very eager to share what they do well and what challenges them in their classrooms. This led to a question that has culminated with the writing of this book: How can I share what I have learned over nearly four decades in a variety of ESL contexts, and how can I include the perspectives of many of my colleagues?

An idea then emerged—why not use a survey to cast a wide net, capitalize on the experiences of my colleagues, weave those responses together with my experiences, and write a book? In 21st-century speak, why not "crowd-source" a book on classroom management? This way, we would have a resource that shares not what someone *believes should* happen in a classroom, but what veteran practitioners *actually do*. Teacher-training programs do a good job of teaching theories like Vygotsky's Zone of Proximal Development and techniques like think-pair-share or peer review. Teachers know they have to use task-based communicative activities and teach students to use before, during, and after strategies when reading. The challenge is how to keep all of these theories and strategies in play as we manage a group of students from a variety of educational and cultural backgrounds. I hoped that the use of a survey, presentation feedback, and conversations with colleagues would allow me to show a range of classroom management techniques from seasoned professionals. Everyone wants a glimpse into how other teachers conduct their classes, and this project gives that opportunity.

The only problem with my idea was finding the time to do such a project. Fast forward a few months to the fall of 2012 when I learned that a President's Sabbatical from my institution, Northern Virginia Community College (NOVA), could give me the time and support that I needed for such a project. In November of 2012 I submitted a proposal that began with this paragraph:

> As I anticipate the celebration of my 20th year of teaching ESL at NOVA and my 37th year in ESL classrooms, I am eager for a period of renewal. The President's Sabbatical offers an incomparable

opportunity for faculty members to reflect on the challenges and rewards of our profession, broaden our experience, and enrich our pedagogical skills. If I am fortunate enough to be selected for a President's Sabbatical Award, I would like to undertake a project to explore best practices in the student-centered classroom, culminating with the publication of a book on ESL classroom management. This project will give me the opportunity to reflect on nearly four decades of professional development, connect and reconnect with current and former colleagues, and share what I learn with a broad audience.

My proposal outlined a three-stage process. In the first stage, I wrote the survey that appears in Appendix 2 of this book. While the survey was being prepared by NOVA's Office of Institutional Research using Qualtrics, I conducted several presentations and workshops, allowing me to have "real time" discussions with dozens of ESL professionals and volunteer teachers. At WATESOL in the fall of 2013 I presented "ESL Classroom Management: Best Practices for Student-Centered Learning," which I structured around six questions such as "What can I do on the first day of class to create a sense of community?" "How can I use modeling effectively?" and "How can kinesthetic activities help my students learn?" Then, on my campus at NOVA, I presented "Moving Toward Learner-Centered Classrooms" in two sessions to teachers in our academic ESL program, our IEP, and our community/adult education program. This presentation examined what it means to move from teacher-centered to student-centered classroom management, from both the teacher's and the students' perspectives. It was exciting to have teachers from all three programs together, sharing in one room.

In January of 2014, I had two more opportunities to present, repeating "ESL Classroom Management: Best Practices for Student-Centered Learning" at a college-wide conference of all six campuses of NOVA and then conducting a two-hour training on "Learner-Centered Instruction in ESL Classrooms" for 50 volunteer teachers at an adult education center in Washington, DC. These opportunities gave me a chance not only to reflect on my own principles but to receive valuable input from teachers at various stages in their careers and who teach in various contexts. Thus, this book is a synthesis of all of these: responses to the survey that appear in Appendix 2, feedback from several presentations, and conversations—in-person or via email—with several colleagues.

Throughout December of 2013 and January of 2014, the survey was "live." I was pleased that so many of my colleagues and friends of colleagues took the time to thoughtfully complete a very long survey. The names of the respondents are listed in the Acknowledgments section of this book, and many of the respondents are quoted throughout the chapters.

After the survey was complete and I had time to consider those responses along with the feedback from my presentations, I continued my information-gathering in emails and conversations with colleagues. In this way I was able to explore some issues that I discovered were not addressed fully in my survey. In addition, I attended TESOL 2014, keeping my ears open for anything related to classroom management and lesson planning. Once back from TESOL, it was time to synthesize my survey responses and conversations, reflect on the style that I have developed over nearly four decades in various classroom contexts, and complete the manuscript.

It should be noted that this is not a book about language teaching techniques or approaches, but rather a way to make techniques work in a classroom of twenty or more individuals. Of course, every teaching situation is a unique crossroads where student backgrounds, needs, and purposes meet a teacher who is ostensibly in control of what happens over a period of weeks or months. And, yes, even in a student-centered environment the teacher is most likely in control. I believe that teacher-centered versus student-centered is a false dichotomy. In a student-centered classroom, the teacher must make important decisions on how to balance teacher-led instruction with pair and group work and whole-class interaction. Classes must contain some amount of instruction, but the skilled teacher knows what students can discover or be responsible for on their own and what needs to be presented in a teacher-centered fashion. This book is intended to allow teachers to develop or hone a style that works in their unique situations.

It should also be noted that this book is more or less a snapshot in time. If I had written this book at the beginning of my career, classroom management might have included ways to structure choral drills, techniques for using "backward buildup" to memorize a dialogue, and hints on getting the most from dittoed grammar exercises! A little later in my career, I might have had to convince teachers to allow students to work in pairs and groups, shifting the focus from linguistic form to communicative competence. In fact, the title of a session I presented at TESOL

1986 was "Communication with Accuracy." I most likely was encouraging teachers to consider using communicative activities and assuring them that they did not have to give up a focus on linguistic form once they gave up their drills! Then the following year, at TESOL 1987, I presented "Developing Student-Centered Activities." This no doubt was a collection of information-gap exercises and "find someone who" activities. A book written in this era may also have urged teachers to consider moving away from fill-in-the-blank, context-free grammar teaching, as evidenced by the title of my 1989 TESOL presentation: "The ESL Grammar Class: Contextualized Exercises, Communicative Activities," and my 1992 TESOL presentation: "The ESL Grammar Class: Introducing Content." A book written at the end of the 1990s might have had large portions devoted to learning styles, considering that my TESOL 1999 presentation was titled "Addressing Multiple Intelligences with Novels" and might also have had a discussion of bringing technology into the classroom, a topic of a 1996 presentation at WATESOL: "No-tech, Lo-tech, Hi-tech: Adapting for Technology."

Now, as a profession, we seem to be comfortably settled into a communicative approach to language teaching, in which the ability to communicate in a variety of modes and using a variety of technologies is seen as the primary focus of our instruction. With that in mind, I asked these questions at the beginning of this project.

- ❏ How can we create a participatory, student-centered classroom environment that fosters the development of language skills?

- ❏ How can we not only craft lesson plans that maximize student engagement but also put those plans into practice?

- ❏ How can we structure interaction between and among students and teachers to individualize instruction and give prompt feedback? How can we maximize time on task while allowing students to work at a comfortable pace?

- ❏ How can we encourage active learning and vary activities to keep classes fresh and interesting without confusing students, or worse, focusing on the activity at hand rather than on the learning that is to be taking place?

My sabbatical was everything I'd hoped for—a time for renewal and a time to reflect on the challenges and rewards of our profession. Eighty colleagues gave hours of their valuable time to complete my survey. Reading their responses and weaving them together into this book has been a great privilege for me; I learn something each and every time I reread what they wrote. I truly hope others enjoy this crowd-sourced work as much as I have.

Acknowledgments

I would like to gratefully acknowledge Northern Virginia Community College (NOVA) for the support that allowed me to complete this project.

I received a President's Sabbatical Award for the spring term of 2014 to complete the bulk of the work for this book. I would like to extend my gratitude for this award to NOVA's president, Dr. Robert G. Templin, Jr.; my dean, Dr. Jim McClellan; as well as to the members of the Personnel Services Committee who recommended my project to Dr. Templin. I would also like to thank my colleague Stephanie Sareeram, who, as a member of the Personnel Services Committee, has been a tireless cheerleader in encouraging applications for the President's Sabbatical Award.

I would like to thank Kelly Sippell of the University of Michigan Press for participating in this project from the beginning. Thank you for being involved since the idea was no more than a "what if?" I am also grateful to the University of Michigan Press reviewers whose comments helped shape the format of the book.

I would also like to acknowledge my colleagues Judy Snyder, Ruth Takushi, and Elisabeth Chan for input into my survey and help with organizing and naming some of the sections of the book.

Thanks also to NOVA's Office of Institutional Research, Planning and Assessment. I would like to acknowledge Dr. George Gabriel for offering the support of OIR and to Saurabh Niraula for creating the online survey and providing me with the data from the responses.

And thank you to my son, Matthew Welborn, for creating the graphics that appear throughout the book.

I would also like to acknowledge the contributions of the many ESL professionals whose names and affiliations are listed. Thank you all for taking the time to fill out my lengthy survey and for all of the email correspondence over the past year. It was a privilege to read your comments. Thank you for opening up the doors to your classrooms!

Finally, a note on NOVA's ESL programs: Many of my colleagues at NOVA contributed to this work. You will note that we work in two large ESL programs across five campuses. Our College ESL program is an EAP program that gives students four semesters of academic preparation before they enter first-year composition. The program enrolls mostly immigrant students, but we also teach international students at our upper levels. Our two upper levels are part-time ESL, offering both reading and composition courses, and our two lower levels are full-time ESL and include oral communication classes along with reading and composition. The American Culture and Language Institute in our Workforce Development Division houses two programs. The Intensive English Program enrolls students at the beginning through intermediate levels. Many of the students in the IEP are on F-1 student visas. The second program, Core Skills ESL, offers part-time courses at many levels for immigrants and students who are in the U.S. temporarily on a variety of visas.

List of Survey Respondents

Brian Anthon	Northern Virginia Community College, College ESL, Alexandria Campus
Wendy Asplin	University of Washington
Laurie Barton	Orange Coast College
Breana Bayraktar	Northern Virginia Community College, College ESL, Woodbridge Campus
Lauren Boone	Harding University
Dan Branch	Northern Virginia Community College, American Culture and Language Institute, Alexandria Campus
Darlene Branges	Northern Virginia Community College, American Culture and Language Institute, Annandale Campus

Acknowledgments xi

Cheri Bridgeforth	Northern Virginia Community College, College ESL, Annandale Campus
Alan Broomhead	Boston University
Virginia A. Cabasa-Hess	Triton College
Megan Calvert	Montgomery College
Nigel Caplan	University of Delaware English Language Institute
Janine Carlock	University of Pittsburgh
Elisabeth Chan	Northern Virginia Community College, College ESL, Alexandria Campus
Mary Charleza	Northern Virginia Community College, College ESL, Annandale Campus
Tracy Bain Chase	Northern Virginia Community College, College ESL, Alexandria Campus
Claire Cirolia	Northern Virginia Community College, College ESL, Alexandria Campus
DeAnna Coon	The Center for Applied Linguistics
Cathy Birdsong Dutchak	Northern Virginia Community College, American Culture and Language Institute, Annandale Campus
Chris Feak	University of Michigan
George A. Flowers	Northern Virginia Community College, College ESL, Manassas Campus
Elaine George	Northern Virginia Community College, College ESL, Manassas Campus
Dorothy Gudgel	Fairfax County Public Schools, ACE Adult Ed ESOL Program

Stephanie Harm	Northern Virginia Community College, College ESL, Woodbridge Campus
Tom Hilanto	The American Language Institute, San Diego State University
W. Riley Holzberlein	Northern Virginia Community College, College ESL, Loudoun Campus
Janice Hornyak	Northern Virginia Community College, College ESL, Alexandria Campus
Carol Ischinger	Northern Virginia Community College, College ESL, Annandale Campus
Dana Kappler	Northern Virginia Community College, College ESL, Alexandria Campus
Gregory Kennerly	The Language Company and Northern Virginia Community College, College ESL, Alexandria Campus
Beverly S. Khabo	Northern Virginia Community College, College ESL, Alexandria Campus
Zaimah Khan	Northern Virginia Community College, College ESL, Loudoun Campus
Therese Kravetz	Florida Southwestern State College
Celia Leckey	Northern Virginia Community College, American Culture and Language Institute, Alexandria Campus
Vivian Leskes	Holyoke Community College
Stephen Lewis	Northern Virginia Community College, American Culture and Language Institute, Annandale Campus
Nina Liakos	Maryland English Institute, University of Maryland College Park

Acknowledgments xiii

Robyn Brinks Lockwood	Stanford University
Christina Luckey	Northern Virginia Community College, College ESL, Alexandria Campus
Agnes Malicka	Northern Virginia Community College, College ESL, Alexandria Campus
Kay Marshall	Northern Virginia Community College, College ESL, Alexandria Campus
Cathleen McCargo	Northern Virginia Community College, American Culture and Language Institute, Alexandria Campus and Georgetown University, TEFL Certificate Program
Jane E. McGinley	Northern Virginia Community College, College ESL, Alexandria Campus and Virginia Tech Language and Culture Institute
Allyson Noble	Falls Church High School, Fairfax County Public Schools
Georgia Mae Oates	Northern Virginia Community College, College ESL, Alexandria Campus
Elizabeth O'Brien	Northern Virginia Community College, American Culture and Language Institute, Alexandria Campus
Marilyn Odaka	Northern Virginia Community College, College ESL, Alexandria Campus
Samantha Parkes	University of Kansas
John Politte	Northern Virginia Community College, American Culture and Language Institute, Annandale Campus
Elizabeth Rasmussen	Northern Virginia Community College, College ESL, Alexandria Campus

Michele Rivera	Northern Virginia Community College, College ESL and English, Loudoun Campus
Antonina N. Rodgers	Northern Virginia Community College, American Culture and Language Institute, Annandale Campus
Peter Ruffner	Northern Virginia Community College, College ESL, Alexandria Campus
Janine Sacramone	Northern Virginia Community College, American Culture and Language Institute, Alexandria Campus
Stephanie Sareeram	Northern Virginia Community College, College ESL, Alexandria Campus
Nataliya Schetchikova	Northern Virginia Community College, College ESL, Annandale Campus
Sherlie Scribner	Northern Virginia Community College, American Culture and Language Institute, Alexandria Campus
Leslie Sheen	Northern Virginia Community College, American Culture and Language Institute, Annandale Campus
Judy Snyder	Northern Virginia Community College, College ESL, Alexandria Campus
Jane Stanga	Northern Virginia Community College, College ESL, Alexandria Campus and Georgetown University, Center for Language Education and Development
Lisa Stelle	Northern Virginia Community College, College ESL, Loudoun Campus
Isabella Strohmeyer	Northern Virginia Community College, College ESL, Loudoun Campus

Acknowledgments xv

Suzanne Mele Szwarcewicz	Acton Boxborough Regional School District
Ruth Takushi	Northern Virginia Community College, College ESL, Alexandria Campus
Shirley Thompson	English Language Training Solutions
Dawn Titafi	Northern Virginia Community College, American Culture and Language Institute, Annandale Campus
Jim Toepper	Northern Virginia Community College, College ESL, Alexandria Campus
Donna M. Tortorella	University of Southern Maine
Til Turner	Northern Virginia Community College, College ESL, Annandale Campus
Karen Van Horn	Northern Virginia Community College, College ESL, Annandale Campus
Albert VanLanduyt	Northern Virginia Community College, American Culture and Language Institute, Annandale Campus
Karen Vlaskamp	Northern Virginia Community College, American Culture and Language Institute, Annandale Campus
Mike J. Waguespack	Northern Virginia Community College, College ESL, Alexandria Campus
Lori Ward	Northern Virginia Community College, College ESL, Alexandria Campus
Kathleen Wax	Northern Virginia Community College, English, Alexandria Campus
Martha Wheeler	Northern Virginia Community College, College ESL, Woodbridge Campus

Elizabeth Whisnant	Northern Virginia Community College, College ESL, Annandale Campus
Rebecca Wolff	Clinton Community College
Bill Woodard	Northern Virginia Community College, College ESL, Manassas Campus

Contents

Introduction	1
Unit One: The Classroom Environment	4
Chapter 1 Setting the Tone in the Classroom	5
Chapter 2 Class Rules	13
The Classroom Environment: Wrap Up	23
Making Connections	24
Unit Two: Lesson Planning in the Student-Centered Classroom	27
Chapter 3 Writing Lesson Plans	28
Chapter 4 Bringing Variety to Lesson Plans	42
Chapter 5 Planning for Student Questions	55
Lesson Planning in the Student-Centered Classroom: Wrap Up	63
Making Connections	65
Unit Three: Pair and Group Work in the Student-Centered Classroom	71
Chapter 6 Pairing and Grouping Students	73
Chapter 7 Integrating Pair and Group Work with Textbook Exercises	82
Chapter 8 Other Pair and Group Opportunities	92
Pair and Group Work in the Student-Centered Classroom: Wrap Up	98
Making Connections	99

Unit Four: Classroom Interactions	102
Chapter 9 **Teacher Places, Teacher Talk**	103
Chapter 10 **Managing Student Interactions**	112
Chapter 11 **Discussion in the Student-Centered Classroom**	130
Classroom Interactions: Wrap Up	139
Making Connections	140
Unit Five: Classroom Trouble Spots	144
Chapter 12 **Arrivals and Breaks**	145
Chapter 13 **Chatting, Helping, Cheating?**	153
Chapter 14 **Smart Phones: Friend or Foe?**	162
Classroom Trouble Spots: Wrap Up	170
Making Connections	172
Appendix 1: Challenging Beliefs	176
Appendix 2: The Survey	186
Appendix 3: Additional Data	198
Index	203

Introduction

Welcome to *Voices of Experience: How Teachers Manage Student-Centered ESL Classes*. This book presents strategies and tips collected through a survey of 80 practicing ESL professionals as well as a series of conversations with my colleagues, seen through the filter of my 38 years in ESL classrooms. Throughout the book, teachers share their motivations for choosing techniques as they give us a look inside their classrooms. A major emphasis throughout is the thinking that underlies teachers' choices in their classroom management strategies.

The book is arranged in five units, with two or three chapters per unit. Survey responses and other input from conversations with colleagues are included throughout the text in direct quotes and in graphics that represent the charts generated by the survey. The complete survey appears in Appendix 2. Please note that in some cases the information in the graphics has been limited to present only the most pertinent data. Readers wishing to view the complete data can find those charts in Appendix 3.

Voices of Experience was designed and written with both novice teachers or teachers-in-training and more seasoned professionals in mind. These two audiences may use the book in slightly different ways, and some parts may resonate more with one group or the other. In essence, newer or future teachers may use the book to look ahead while veterans use it to look around.

At the end of each unit, Making Connections presents several opportunities for reflection or discussion. Practicing teachers may want to simply reflect on those parts or use them for discussion in brown-bag lunches with their colleagues, or they may use the material to engage in more formal in-service professional development. Students in ESL methods courses or practicum programs may use the material for class discussion, response papers, or journal topics. Each Making Connections section includes:

- **Challenging Beliefs: What Teachers Think.** Readers react to a statement using a Likert scale and then can turn to Appendix 1 to see how teachers responded to that statement on the survey. Here readers will find selected comments showing the range of opinions of those surveyed. Practicing teachers may wish to measure their opinions against what others said, while future teachers may use the comments as a springboard for discussion or writing. For example, they may be asked to select the comment that most closely matches their opinion and explain why in a short paper or journal entry.

- **Classroom Connections: What Teachers Do.** Readers find a list of eight to ten questions to connect the topics in the unit with an actual classroom. Practicing teachers may use these questions to think about how they manage their classes or as a framework to guide their observation of classes taught by colleagues or teachers whom they are supervising. Future teachers may use these questions to guide their observations of ESL classes or to reflect on their teaching practicum experiences in a journal, for example.

- **Strategies and Motivations: What Teachers Say.** Readers consider quotes from survey respondents on some of the topics covered in the unit. Some quotes are pithy bits of wisdom, while longer quotes are included as teachers explain their underlying motivations for the choices they make in their classrooms. In short, these quotations show how good teaching is a balance of art and science. Practicing teachers may reflect on these additional glimpses into their colleagues' classrooms, while future teachers may choose one of these ways to interact with the quotes in this section:
    - Choose two of the quotes that you think give good advice and tell why you like the advice. Does this describe what you do or would do in your classroom?

- Choose one or more quotes for reflection. What questions come to mind? Formulate a question or questions about the strategies or motivations that you might ask a practicing teacher.
- Choose two or more quotes for a response. You may choose two that seem similar and reflect on how they are similar or two that seem different and reflect on how both teachers are successful with different strategies and motivations.

I am certainly not the same teacher I was 38 years ago, and I am not even the same teacher I was 38 weeks ago. Reflecting on the input that I received in the course of this project has given me new perspectives on my classroom dynamic. A teaching career is a journey, and we never stop developing. I hope that in some way this book is a valuable tool for each reader's journey.

Janet Giannotti
Arlington, VA, 2015
B.S. Georgetown University
M.A. The University of South Florida
M. Ed. The University of Virginia

Unit One:
The Classroom Environment

In a student-centered classroom, we see learners actively using or manipulating English as they are involved in activities or working through exercises, often in pairs and groups. Many activities are collaborative, and a great deal of communication takes place in the target language as students interact with and rely on their peers. However, students may not come to their ESL class expecting to do this. They certainly expect to develop a relationship with their teacher, but they probably do not come to an ESL class expecting to develop relationships with their peers. However, this is a necessary part of learning a second language. Language is a social construct, and interaction using the language is essential for acquisition. It is the teacher's responsibility to make this happen.

Most teachers seek to create a learner-centered environment for their students, but this does not mean the teacher sits back and lets students "run the show." In a learner-centered classroom, the teacher balances teacher-led instruction with opportunities for students to discover on their own. She determines when pair or group work will be used and manages those situations. Depending on their backgrounds, our ESL students may find this environment new and confusing.

Given a possible conflict between expectations and goals, it is important to set the right tone in our classes. This unit deals with what we do in the first few classes of a session and how we create and communicate classroom rules.

Chapter 1
Setting the Tone in the Classroom

Most teachers believe that it is important to set the tone of the class early on. This chapter deals with creating the right atmosphere in the first week or two of the course.

Figure 1

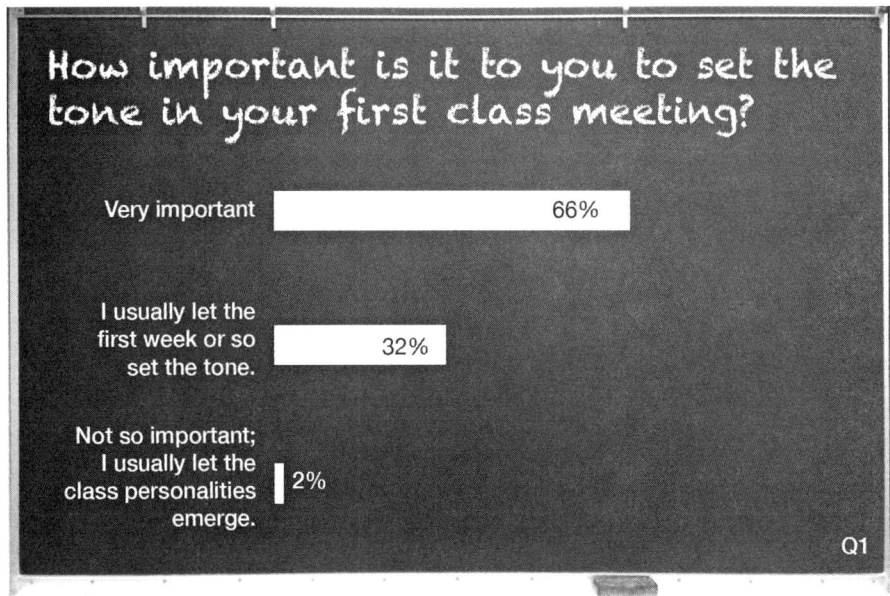

Icebreakers

Teachers often use some kind of get-to-know-you or icebreaker activity in the first or second class meeting. These activities can serve several purposes in setting the class tone and getting started with instruction. They tell students that they matter as part of a learning community, make students feel comfortable, and show them what they have in common with their classmates. They also help teachers gain valuable information on students' backgrounds, their lives (are they working? do they have families?), their goals or purpose for being in the class, and some of their strengths and weaknesses.

It should also be noted that some teachers do not use an icebreaker in the **first** class. Some icebreakers may seem like games, and we don't want our students to think they enrolled in our class to play games. Instead, many teachers use the first class for diagnostic testing and save an icebreaker for the second day. Doing this communicates high expectations: The students know that the teacher wants to evaluate their academic skills right away. Another strategy is to weave some instruction into the icebreaker to show students that they can learn while engaged in a task. In a class that meets for two or more hours, I usually like to accomplish all three: some assessment, some instruction (even something as simple as what a heading looks like in MLA format), and some icebreaker with a homework assignment that develops from the icebreaker.

> "Students are most excited about a class on the first meeting; make it great. A more than usual amount of 'housekeeping' tasks might be expected, but also plan an activity that really gives students a taste of what's to come. Let them leave having learned something."
>
> *Darlene Branges*

Many teachers' go-to icebreaker is to put students in pairs, ask them to interview each other, and then stand up to introduce their partners. These introductions should be kept short, especially in large classes. Students can be encouraged to tell one interesting fact about their partner, for example. Another strategy for this activity is to ask students to find out what they have in common with their partner. This lends some focus to the interview and introduction and is a simple and effective first step for turning a group of strangers into a community of learners.

It's also a good idea to get students out of their seats in the first class or two, especially if they have been sitting for a long time listening to the teacher or taking diagnostic tests. Many teachers like to use a Find Someone Who activity, either in a list or on a bingo board. These work well in the second class meeting; you can use what you learn about your students in the first meeting to construct the activity.

Some of us like to have students stand in a circle on the first or second day of class as well. Students can arrange themselves in the order of their birth month, or alphabetically by their first names or the name of their home country. While they are standing, they may simply introduce themselves, or you may challenge them to memorize their classmates' names (as each student introduces himself, he repeats the names of all of the students who went before him). I usually tell my students that they need to see each other's faces right away, as communication doesn't take place while one is looking at the back of the other person's head. I tell them on the first day that they'll be working together in every class session, so it's important for me to have them meet each other as quickly as possible.

> **Cathleen McCargo notes** that "establishing classroom community in the initial classes is extremely important." She writes that she "allows students an opportunity to learn about each other through structured pair interviews."

Other icebreakers allow students to share more about themselves. Some teachers ask students to discuss their names (perhaps what their name means or the significance of their name in their family or culture). Others ask students to write their names on cards or name tags and write four interesting facts about themselves in the four corners of the card before mingling and talking. And other teachers like to play Two Truths and a Lie.

If you use Two Truths and a Lie, it is best to start with yourself, not only to model the activity but also as one way to introduce yourself to the class. In fact, allowing the students to learn a little about you while you learn about them is important in setting the tone. Besides Two Truths and a Lie, I have recently been asking students to brainstorm questions for me in groups. I tell them they can ask me anything, but they usually don't get too personal. Once each group has brainstormed at least three questions, the class comes back together and they ask me the questions.

I usually follow up with a writing assignment for homework: Students write a letter to a classmate who was absent, telling that student a little about me.

Rebecca Wolff reports that if she has a student who already knows her from a previous class, she has that student introduce her. She writes, "It is fun to see how much they remember about me, and it also opens up the class to questions and creates a comfortable tone."

> **Megan Calvert introduces** herself in an activity that gets students ready to interview each other: "I write answers to questions about me that I want my students to know in a web around my name, and the students have to guess the questions. There's lots of opportunity for silly jokes, and it helps them think of questions they can ask their partners in a subsequent interview activity."

And, finally, some icebreakers can ask students to stretch their thinking skills. One that I have used asks students to dig into their backpacks, purses, or wallets and to pull out three items. They then tell what those three items *symbolize* about themselves. I always model this first. I pull out my key ring, which has only two keys on it, my driver's license, which qualifies me to ride a motorcycle, and my business card. I tell students, these show that I value a simple life, I like to take risks, and I love my job! I usually have students share their objects in groups, and then ask each group to report on one or two interesting objects to the class. This gives me the chance to say, over and over, "Yes, but what does that *symbolize* about you? How does that object tell us who you *are*?" Then the students write short essays about their objects/themselves. I like this because it pushes students in my upper-level composition class to think in an abstract way in the very first week, and it tells me who has this ability as well as who might need more of my attention as we move along.

In another activity to stretch students' thinking skills, Lori Ward likes to ask students to come up with three items they would need to live on a desert island. She uses a think-pair-share strategy, allowing students to come up with a list on their own, to share the list with a group and then again with the whole class. The discussion that develops shows students that, in her class, "it's being resourceful that will be most important in helping students 'survive' the semester!" An activity like this also gives you, the teacher, an opportunity to praise students' creative thinking—an important strategy for setting students up for success early on.

In fact, it's a good idea to set students up for success in any first-week activity. Keep the task simple and gauge the students' comfort level before launching into an activity. If you don't think your students will be comfortable sharing personal information on the first day, construct your activity with that in mind. If you create an atmosphere of trust at the outset, students will be willing to take risks and share on a more personal level later on.

And one final consideration: Whatever you choose as an icebreaker, it's important to consider whether your students are taking only your class or whether they are enrolled in two or more ESL classes at your school. If they are enrolled in more than one class, keep in mind that they are doing icebreakers in their other class(es) as well, and if they are continuing students who have been in your program before, they have surely done icebreakers before. This makes it important to "change it up" and use different icebreakers in different semesters and with different skills! Imagine how boring it must be to interview a partner three or more times in one week!

> "I always make sure the icebreaker activity uses the skills in the class title. For example, students do a reading and writing activity for a reading and writing class. I always make sure the activity involves communicating with their classmates and sharing that information with the entire class."
>
> *Janine Sacramone*

Learning Names

If our students only knew how hard we work to learn their names! ESL teachers clearly understand the importance of calling people by their names in a learner-centered environment, and they know how much it matters to students that they know them as people. But learning so many names in a short time is a challenge! Teachers report many strategies for quickly learning students' names.

First, it's a good idea to review your roster before you go to class. If your institution provides a photo roster, that is a big help! Then when you call the roll in the first class, ask the students to correct your pronunciation or to let you know if there is another name such as a nickname that they'd like to be called. Repeat each student's name, and if necessary make a note in IPA (or a similar phonological system) on your roster of how to pronounce it. Showing students an eagerness to learn creates an atmosphere of "we are all in this together."

Some teachers like to have students wear name tags or to write their names in large letters on a "tent" for their desk. This works well to get you started, but students will surely lose their tents, and you won't want to use a lot of class time collecting and distributing them, so you have to memorize the names at some point.

> **Elizabeth Rasmussen** takes pictures of small groups of students at their desks, holding their name tents. Of course students can opt out of the picture, but so far she reports that no one has. She relaxes students by telling them something like, "Ali, pretend you are telling the other two how to stay awake in class." That usually makes them laugh while she's photographing them. Then she tells them learning their names is her homework for the next class.

Most teachers use a variety of tricks to memorize names. I seem to be able to remember names if I associate name + country + hair. However, this got me in trouble early in my career when I taught a particular group of students—all female, all from Malaysia, all with their hair covered with scarves. I admit I never learned their names! More recently, I'm usually fine until someone changes a hair style or wears a hat!

Many teachers report that making a note of a physical feature helps them remember students' names. Look for something distinctive about the student and make a note of it. Really look at each student's face. You can watch them and quiz yourself while they are completing a diagnostic test and they probably won't notice!

> "I test myself after breaks and at the beginning of class by trying to say all their names aloud in front of the class. It's fun for them to watch their teacher be a learner, and it shows them that I care."
>
> *Megan Calvert*

Another strategy is to use a seating chart. You can assign seats, but usually students will tend to sit in the same general part of the room—especially in the first week or two. Our ability to form spatial memories is quite strong! Georgia Mae Oates reports, "For some reason, my students usually sit in the same spots for the first few sessions, and in my mind's eye their name appears in the air above that spot!"

> Elisabeth Chan offers this clever tip: Associate the student's name with his or her backpack. "They may change their clothes and seats, but usually their backpack stays the same."

Once you are on the road to learning the names, say the students' names as much as possible, and have them call each other by their names, or recall each other's names for you. Assign some written work in the first few classes. When students turn it in, you can say, "Thank you, [name]." When you are ready to hand papers back to the students, don't have students pick up their own papers. Instead, pass them back, trying your best to match the papers to the students (handwriting gives me another important visual cue!), and say the students' names aloud. Tell them you are trying to learn their names. Apologize for mistakes. Showing students that everyone works hard to learn, and that everyone makes mistakes when they are learning, helps to set the right tone in your class.

> "**Encourage students** to call each other by name. Also, help students learn to pronounce their names in an 'American English-friendly way' by using only the sounds of English and having one clear, primary stress. This is a great pronunciation lesson!"
>
> *Shirley Thompson*

A crucial first step in creating a student-centered classroom is setting the tone in the first few class meetings. Teachers ensure that everyone gets to know each other as quickly as possible to create a collaborative atmosphere. Teachers learn students' names and personalities as they assess their strengths and weaknesses with English and begin instruction.

Chapter 2
Class Rules

Student-centered classes that require active participation and in which students rely on each other for much of their learning must be governed by clear rules that are understood by all. While a large lecture-hall university course may have one or two rules (e.g., turn cell phones off, no talking while the professor is lecturing), student-centered classrooms need a few more rules to work smoothly.

The Golden Rule

Class rules create a positive learning environment in student-centered classes. Most rules are presented as dos rather than as don'ts. The number one rule that most teachers report is: **respect everyone.** In the spirit of "show, don't tell," most teachers try to elicit examples of how we respect each other from their students. Suzanne Mele Szwarcewicz asks students to talk through what is meant by respect in a classroom. She reports that students usually come up with "listening to others, respecting people's time and opinions, and being prepared."

Many teachers describe class rules that illustrate how to show respect in a student-centered environment, as this concept might be new to students who are used to more teacher-centered instruction. Students who come from cultures in which respect is shown by, for example, rising when the teacher enters the room are often a little surprised by what we mean by respect.

The first rule that many teachers report is to listen when other people speak. And this means, listen to your classmates as well as to the teacher. Don't talk when someone else is talking, even in a whispered side-bar conversation.

Next, be kind to your classmates; treat them as colleagues or friends. Be tolerant of everyone's beliefs. Ruth Takushi points out that some students need to learn that "different is not wrong; it's just different."

Teachers also point out that students may have to learn how to disagree respectfully.

Another way to show respect is by being an active participant in the class. This, again, may be in conflict with what students have been taught in many years of education in different contexts. In a student-centered environment, everyone shares responsibility for learning. Accepting this shared responsibility means that everyone must come to class ready to learn—with materials, pencils, paper, and, most important, with homework completed on time. Coming to class prepared generally means getting into a regular study routine and being organized. Students who find the homework difficult must at least make an attempt to complete it; nothing slows down a group faster than an unprepared participant.

> **Therese Kravetz notes** that the rules in her classroom are there to tell students that "it's safe to share your opinion." She adds that "an atmosphere of trust is most important."

Regular and punctual attendance is also a way of showing respect to the class and the teacher. Many teachers expect a phone call or an email if a student is absent, and many have rules about not giving make-up tests in order to encourage regular attendance; they drop the lowest test or quiz score to allow for the occasional sick day. Many teachers allow a little grace period if a student is late but encourage late comers to slip in quietly. Finally, many teachers note that unauthorized breaks are a problem, so they have rules about not leaving class for a coffee or cigarette break.

Another set of rules that teachers report concerns taking responsibility for learning. Teachers stress that students must ask if they don't understand something. They must be responsible for reading and following directions and for checking email and other online sources such as the course management system. Many teachers have stringent requirements about the formatting of written work, including emails. They find that if they have high expectations, students will rise to them and produce work they can be proud of. As Tom Hilanto puts it, students need to understand that how much they learn is "a reflection of how hard they work, especially the time and effort spent outside of regular classroom meetings."

> **Gregory Kennerly reports** on one important rule in his classroom: "At the end of class, do NOT leave the classroom not knowing what to do. Ask a question or two. Do not go home confused."

Teachers also have a couple of don'ts on their lists of rules. These include, of course, no cell phones. Why we even need to say this is obvious when we realize that people use their cell phones at work, while they shop, on buses, in their cars, in restaurants, in theaters—everywhere. So while students may not be expecting to chat with a friend while in class, they may forget to turn the phones off and may need a rule as a reminder. Stephanie Sareeram has her classes vote on a "consequence" for a violation of the cell phone rule. She reports that if a cell phone rings in her class, "usually the perpetrator brings food."

> **"I don't have specific rules**, but I do a very big sell on taking responsibility for their own learning. I give students several ways to contact me, including by text message, so they take the lead in solving any issues. In other words, NO EXCUSES. From the start, I promote professional behavior and I make references to real job scenarios."
>
> *Tracy Bain Chase*

Other don'ts: No dictionaries unless the class activity calls for dictionary use, no cheating or copying of someone's homework, no plagiarism, and no begging or negotiations. And, yes, we might need to explicitly state these rules in many of our classes, although sometimes we wait to see if the issues arise, as we don't really want to start the session with a lot of negatives. However, some students have an unhealthy relationship with their dictionaries or say, "I'm on my phone looking up a word" as a cover for texting a friend or using social media. Some students are so eager to please the teacher but so busy outside of class that they turn to copying their homework from a classmate just to have something to turn in. And the definition of what constitutes plagiarism varies from culture to culture, so this is often a large learning curve for our students. Finally, creating a comfortable relationship between students and teacher may lead students to overstep the boundary and feel that they can negotiate a better grade or beg for a second chance. Being kind but firm usually takes care of this issue.

Communicating Rules

In my survey, two-thirds of respondents reported communicating rules via a syllabus on the first day of class (see Figure 2). They clearly believe in establishing expectations right away.

It should be noted that simply handing a syllabus to a class—or posting it in an online forum—is not going to automatically lead to student buy-in on class rules. Teachers report having students engage with their class rules in a variety of ways through the first weeks of the session. For example, Cathleen McCargo describes how she ensures that her students are connecting with the course documents: "At the bottom of the syllabus, there is a space for students to sign and date. This ensures that they have read the information and that they agree to its terms."

Figure 2

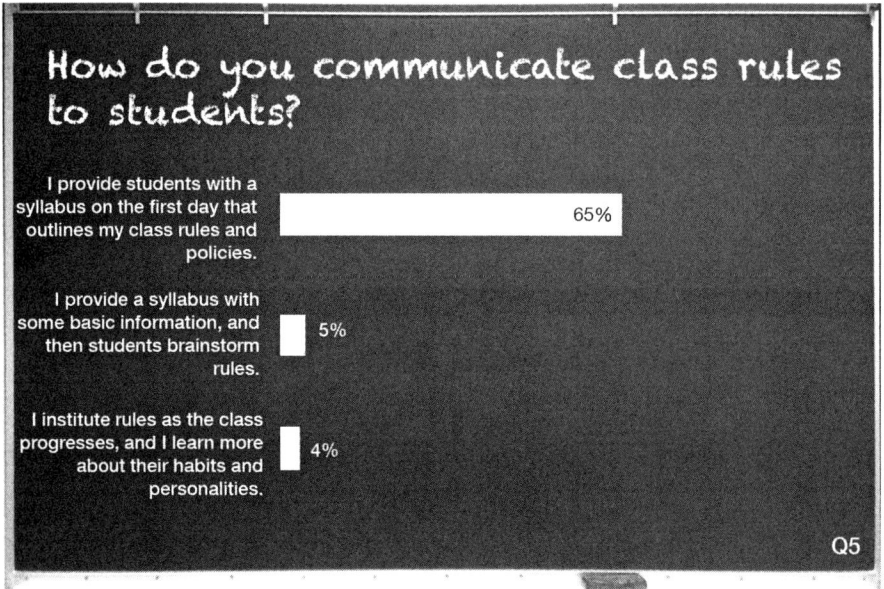

Note: Additional responses to this item appear in Appendix 3.

Many teachers also use syllabus quizzes or other activities. Lisa Stelle reports that she "provides the syllabus on Day One, and we play 'Syllabus Seek-and-Find' on Day Two to help the students learn more about the policies. A syllabus quiz a week later ties everything together."

I tried something fun recently—syllabus speed-dating! I had twenty students. On the second day of class, I got to the classroom early and arranged the desks in two lines of ten, facing each other. To the desks that faced the door, I taped copies of the syllabus (which students had been asked to read for homework). Ten students sat in those chairs; we'll call them Group A. The other ten—Group B—sat in the opposite chairs, and I gave each one of them a sheet with ten questions on it, such as "What should I do if I miss a class?" and "What will happen if I copy my classmate's homework and turn it in as if I wrote it myself?" As the activity started, I asked the partners to introduce themselves, and Group B asked Group A the first question, making a note of the answer. I watched the clock for about three minutes, and then yelled "Group B: Move!" Group B moved one desk to the right, with the last person running back to the beginning, and the pattern repeated with the second question. Yes, it was chaos the first few moves! It was a lot to ask a brand new group to do on Day Two, but it accomplished what I wanted. The class reviewed ten important points on the syllabus, everyone got to meet at least ten new people, and the student-centered nature of the class was illustrated quite effectively.

> **Jane Stanga's** approach for generating class rules is to ask students to "work in pairs or small groups to solve case study problems related to the rules. For example, "'Mo is 20 minutes late to every class. What might be the consequences of Mo's behavior?'"

In addition to explaining rules, some teachers find it useful to ask students to generate their own rules. For example, Kay Marshall reports, "Our class rules are in the information sheet distributed on the first day of class, but I also try to get students to buy into them by asking what they think important classroom rules should be." Megan Calvert notes, "With adult students, I find it best to just institute some basic rules and expectations on the first day and then democratically add rules as needed. With teenagers, I think the process of having them create their own rules is valuable because it helps them explore and grow, and it gives them buy-in into the rules."

Many teachers report that class rules sometimes have to be amended, often weeks into the session. If you note some problem areas such as late arrivals, breaks that grow longer and longer each day, or pockets of friends who sit together and start to socialize, you can institute new rules—most successfully with the students' input. Similarly, some rules can be relaxed if you see the class is running smoothly. For example, a "no breaks" rule might be amended to "you may slip out to visit the restroom as long as you do not interrupt the flow of the class."

And, finally, when I discuss class rules with my students, my last question to them is usually, "How much time do you think you need to spend on homework for this class?" While this is not a "rule" as such, it is healthy to discuss this expectation early on in the semester when students still have a chance to arrange schedules. Of course, some students work faster than others, and this should also be discussed. Homework time should be expressed in ranges. You might say, "You should spend five to ten hours per week for my class. If you are spending less or more time, please talk to me about your homework strategies."

Rules are like an umbrella that makes the classroom a safe place for everyone so that they can take the risks they need to in order to learn. Being clear about rules early on and involving students in the creation and later amendment of rules is a cornerstone of a student-centered classroom.

English-Only Policies

When asked about their class rules, very few teachers surveyed reported having an English-only rule in their classes. As previously described, rules were mostly about respecting each other, having respect for class time, and about taking responsibility for learning.

However, when asked directly about allowing use of students' L1, two-thirds of respondents reported English-only policies (see Figure 3).

While the majority reported having an English-only policy, in their notes many teachers referred to unwritten or flexible policies about allowing the use of students' L1. This is clearly an issue that must be decided with your students and your program.

If I had taken this survey as a new teacher, I most certainly would have reported having an English-only policy. When I was a graduate

Figure 3

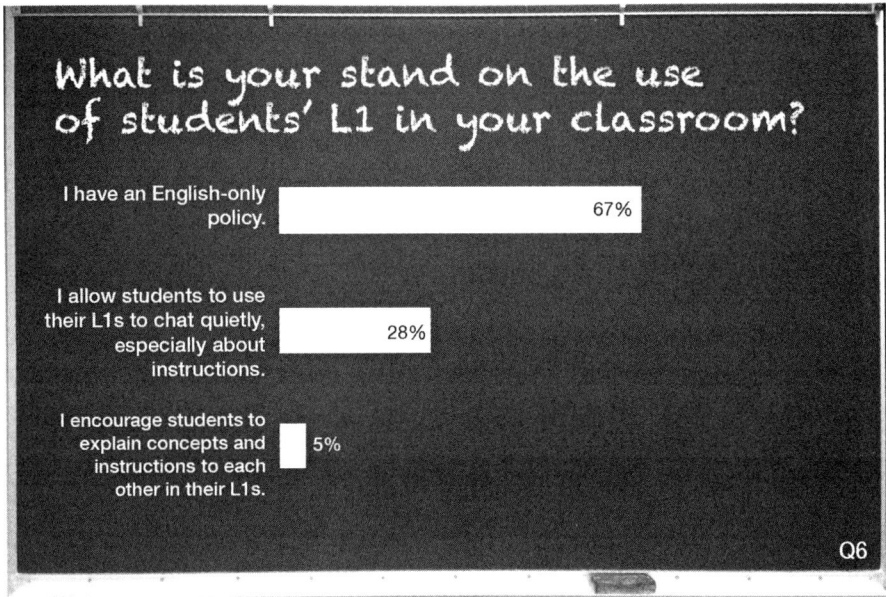

student I taught in my university's IEP. The program had a very diverse student population, so I don't know why I was so concerned, but I distinctly recall having a coffee can on my desk into which students deposited a quarter each time they broke my rule and spoke in their L1. We used the collected money for a pizza party at the end of the semester. I think I began questioning this policy the day a student arrived for class, stuffed a dollar into the can, and said, "I'm tired today and I know I'll be using a lot of Arabic!"

Today I would probably choose choice #2 (see Figure 3): I don't have any specific prohibition against students' L1 use. While I hear myself saying "Only English, please!" in a noisy classroom, this is more of an assumption that my students come to the college to speak English than a stated rule. I'm sure my students come to class expecting to be asked to speak in English, but I'm not comfortable prohibiting the use of their first languages while mandating only the use of *my* first language. I feel that this sets me up as the holder of power in the room. I think students can be empowered as learners by allowing some use of their L1s in the classroom, especially if we view our goal as fostering bilingualism. My goal is not to replace their L1 with English but to layer English on top of their L1. In short, I don't want to label my students' L1 as "bad."

> "I have an unwritten English-only policy. In other words, it is not stated in the syllabus or other official document. It is more my expectation that students will avoid speaking their L1s with others primarily because they are enrolled in an ENGLISH class. I will reprimand students in their L1 when possible. I think it sends a message that I can understand and communicate, and it surprises them. For others, I often simply remind them that it is their time and money to spend wisely."
>
> *Jim Toepper*

If we can see this from a student's perspective, we might have a more flexible policy about English-only rules. Alan Broomhead reports on some research with students on their attitudes toward English-only rules. He notes that "students experience English-only in a variety of ways. Most embrace the idea but most also struggle with it." Take, for example, a student who is new to the country who has joined an Intensive English Program with classmates from several other countries. While we may do our best to create a welcoming environment in which we stress what students have in common with each other, we need to realize that our students are sitting in a group of virtual strangers, and that we are asking them to make mistakes in front of those strangers. In addition, they may come from EFL environments that don't prepare them for the kind of informal interaction that we expect in our classrooms. To survive in this situation, Alan Broomhead writes that students "may struggle to express themselves without reference to their first language, or they may not be able to remain attentive to a constant stream of English, which may also overwhelm them at times. Many students seem to be mentally translating or formulating in their first language before speaking or writing. Many of them 'think in their first language' or use first language resources such as a bilingual dictionary." Thus, while we may believe we are creating an English-only environment by prohibiting our students from speaking in their L1, it is never really English-only for our students.

That said, we often work in programs that mandate only English in our classrooms, as students come to the United States with some expectation that speaking only English is the best way to learn. As Wendy Asplin points out, "Students appreciate the English-only rule, even those who violate it." But as Alan Broomhead notes, "While the teacher is employing one strategy to teach—English only—for many students the experience continues to be a bilingual one in which they struggle with language and struggle to reconcile their bilingual language use with the monolingual classroom rule."

> **Peter Ruffner explains,** "I believe that having a strict English-only policy can inhibit students. I think it's counter-productive to reprimand students for uttering a few sentences to a classmate in their L1. However, when it comes to group work, I try to put students from different language backgrounds together."

Indeed, an English-only policy is perhaps the most violated rule in many programs. Several teachers reported that their programs generally have English-only policies but that they bend that rule at times. They report being flexible, and relaxing the rule when it's beneficial. Some teachers try to create an English-only space in the classroom but allow or encourage use of L1s during breaks (which are just that—breaks from the mental stress of thinking and negotiating in a second language.) To this point, Alan Broomhead found in his study that "students with the same first language confer with each other in that language, sometimes behind the teacher's back or when the teacher is out of the room. Many students seem to need to take breaks from English by speaking their first language with their classmates." In fact, some teachers report orchestrating same-L1 groups after a challenging assignment to allow students to discuss how it felt to work strictly in their L2. These groups can meet outside of your classroom if you want to keep your room an English-only space. But since lower-level students report that they just can't express complex thoughts in English, and since learning English is indeed an important endeavor for our students, it seems logical to encourage students to talk about the process in a comfortable (L1) setting.

Many teachers don't have explicit English-only rules. They report that they urge students to use only English—more so at higher levels when they should be able to express complex thoughts in their L2 and less so at lower levels—but allow occasional translation if that helps move the class ahead. Of course, English-only rules are more necessary when the class members speak one or a couple of native languages. In classes with a mix of native languages, it isn't hard to pair or group students so that it's necessary to communicate in English. Personally, I think if the use of L1s got out of hand in one of my classes, I would certainly address this with a new rule or amended rule, as was suggested in the previous section. In fact, it is essential that we include students in the conversation about our class language policy. We often need to take into consideration our students' learning processes when we institute or change rules about their use of L1s in the classroom, and to create rules with understanding, empathy, and sensitivity.

In general, we want students to be focused on the task of learning English, and we craft policies to that end. As Ruth Takushi points out, "Even if we don't know the language the students are using, we can usually tell if they are on task. If they are on task, I encourage the use of English, but I don't force it."

> **Brian Anthon points out** one caveat in allowing use of L1s: "Students without a common L1 may feel slighted if L1 help is not available to them but is available to others in the class." He prefers an English-only environment in which "instructors know they need to scaffold, model, and clarify for student success. Part of the learning process involves a student's requirement to ask for addition input from the instructor if comprehension is blocked. Having a peer or even the instructor translate to L1 prolongs the learning process."

In a student-centered environment, rules including policies about the use of students' first languages are generally crafted with an eye toward moving the students forward in their acquisition of English. If students know the rules and understand why they are in place, the class should run smoothly. Similarly, if teachers empathize with students and see the rules through the students' eyes, creating and amending them collaboratively, then student-centered learning can thrive.

The Classroom Environment: Wrap-Up

Students often come to their first ESL class in the United States expecting to develop a relationship with their teacher, but they often do not expect that they have to create a relationship with their classmates in order for language skills to develop. There must be a sense of reciprocity, of reciprocal teaching, in the classmates' relationship with each other, and it is the teacher who fosters this.

A student-centered classroom is not in fact the opposite of a teacher-centered classroom. In a student-centered classroom, the teacher is not simply a passive participant: Teachers have to create a safe and respectful environment that is at the same time rigorous and challenging to students. They do this by taking into consideration students' backgrounds and lives outside of class, their expectations, and their goals. They first create a community of learners and then create and implement rules within which the class functions. They show sensitivity when instituting rules and crafting policies about the use of students' first languages, taking into consideration students' perspectives. In creating such environments, teachers show students that they are mutually responsible for everyone's learning.

Making Connections

Challenging Beliefs: What Teachers Think

What's your opinion? Circle the extent to which you agree or disagree with this statement. To read survey responses to the statement, please turn to Appendix 1 (pages 176–177).

> I find it hard to strike the right balance between being approachable and friendly and being respected as an authority in the room.
>
> strongly agree   agree   neither agree nor disagree   disagree   strongly disagree

Classroom Connections: What Teachers Do

In a class you are teaching or visiting, you may want to consider some of these points about what happens in the first week or so of the session.

1. Are the students engaged in an icebreaker?
2. Do students interview and introduce each other?
3. Is there a strategy to help the teacher and students learn everyone's name?
4. Is there an opportunity for the students to get to know a little about the teacher?
5. Is diagnostic testing carried out? If so, how are results communicated to students?
6. Are students engaging with the syllabus or other written course materials?
7. Are class rules discussed?
8. Is the use of students' first languages permitted, or is this issue discussed?

Strategies and Motivations: What Teachers Say

Consider these comments from survey respondents on a few of the topics from this unit.

On being sensitive on the first day:

Sometimes we need to put ourselves in our students' shoes. Our classrooms are comfortable places for us as teachers, but remember that being in a classroom may be a very new experience for some of our students.

> George Flowers: "I find many students are mortified standing up to introduce themselves in front of a room of strangers — especially in a second language."

On the importance of learning and using students' names:

Recently I was teaching a spelling class. It was a small group of about 15 students, and we only met three hours a week. While we did a lot of pair work and I called out students' names as I returned work, I hadn't been good about *making* students learn everyone's name. Around mid-term, I was having students work in groups and overheard two students introducing themselves to each other. I was embarrassed and apologized to the group for not doing a better job creating a sense of community.

> Darlene Branges: "Learn everyone's name as soon as possible and use their names often. Using names builds community which in turn creates a comfortable learning environment. Never asking students their names makes them feel unimportant or invisible to the instructor and to each other. Classmates may still feel like strangers in the middle of the semester."

On class rules:

As was discussed in this chapter, most class rules focus on the creation of a respectful environment: respect for fellow students and the teacher, respect for a variety of cultures and opinions, and respect for time.

Rebecca Wolff: "The most important rule in my classroom is mutual respect. I want students to feel comfortable and confident that if they challenge themselves (and make a mistake), they will not be made fun of by others. Teaching students to listen to each other is important."

Cathleen McCargo: "Respect for each other is the most important classroom rule. Tolerance and cooperation are the other rules that are reiterated as students work to create a strong classroom community."

On the use of students' first languages in the classroom:

We know that students come to an English class expecting to use English. But we also know that students need to employ a variety of strategies when acquiring a new language, and bridging from L1 to L2 may work as one of those strategies. That said, deciding when and how to allow use of students' L1 in the classroom means that teachers have to make judgment calls, often on the spot.

Elaine George: "While I prefer students to use English, I don't see the point of wasting precious class time trying to explain a difficult concept if a quick translation will do the job. There is a fine line, though. If certain students are constantly using their L1, I ask them to use English."

Judy Snyder: "I do not absolutely forbid the use of students' L1, but I encourage the use of English mainly so that no one feels uncomfortable. This is especially important if a class has a large number of students who speak the same language."

Alan Broomhead: "While English-only might seem to be a useful practice for creating harmony in the classroom by having everyone use the same language, in reality the disharmony doesn't disappear from the classroom, but is 'pushed inside' or 'pushed under the surface' where students have to deal with it themselves, especially if the teacher hasn't made the role and use of the first language a topic of classroom conversation and thereby legitimized it as something that can be discussed by the students there."

Unit Two:
Lesson Planning in the Student-Centered Classroom

A student-centered ESL class, unlike a college or university lecture class, is often made up of a variety of activities, often in a progression. This makes the topic of lesson planning perhaps more relevant in an ESL (or other foreign language) context than in other subject areas. ESL teachers are tasked with planning lessons that weave some amount of explicit instruction with a variety of practice—individual, in pairs, and in groups. Students expect and appreciate some direct instruction on a regular basis, no matter what the skill area. However, it's easy to fall into a trap of too much teacher talk—too much explaining or even "performing"—without turning over some responsibility to the learners. It's also easy to fall into the trap of too much group work or pair work, especially with unstructured assignments or open-ended discussion. Thus, careful planning is essential.

Novice teachers or volunteers who are sent into classrooms with little training are often taught a lesson-plan template that is suitable for their context. In addition, some textbooks in essence "teach themselves," as instructors and students move from exercise to exercise through a chapter. However, as tempting as it might be to see lesson planning as plugging activities into a template or completing four pages of a text per class, we cannot leave the decisions about what we do, how long we spend on each activity, and the order in which to conduct our classes to a template or to a textbook.

This unit deals with creating plans, flexibility in planning, bringing a variety of activities into classes, and planning for and encouraging student questions.

Chapter 3
Writing Lesson Plans

One of my rituals at the beginning of every session is a shopping trip to buy notebooks for my lesson plans. I look forward to designing and planning each course I teach, with my new notebook a blank slate onto which I map a new session. I think I'm not alone in my love of having a fresh start two or three times a year. Teachers understand the value of crafting and revising good plans for student-centered learning. This chapter deals with writing lesson plans, with advice on how and how much to plan.

Writing Your Plan

Teachers-in-training may be required to write detailed lesson plans for their professors or mentors to check, but as teachers gain more experience, do they stop having to write down their plans? The short answer to this question is no: 78 percent of respondents reported that they write out a plan "always" or "most of the time" (see Figure 4). When it comes to writing their class plans, teachers seem to fall along a continuum. On one end, some teachers plan several weeks or even their whole semester in advance, allowing more time to grade papers week by week. Others have taught the same class several times and need barely a note or two before going to class.

Most teachers fall somewhere in the middle of the continuum. They write a plan before each class, which may be anything from a few notes to a more elaborate plan. Many teachers report having an outline or a list of topics with notes about page numbers, homework, and any administrative issues that need to be addressed. Some teachers report preparing handouts, PowerPoints, or other visuals before going to class, but they don't generally write out what they are going to say verbatim. I often come up with the examples I want to use in a grammar explanation and write them in my plan, for example. Some teachers make notes of how long each part of the lesson should take. I find, even many years

Figure 4

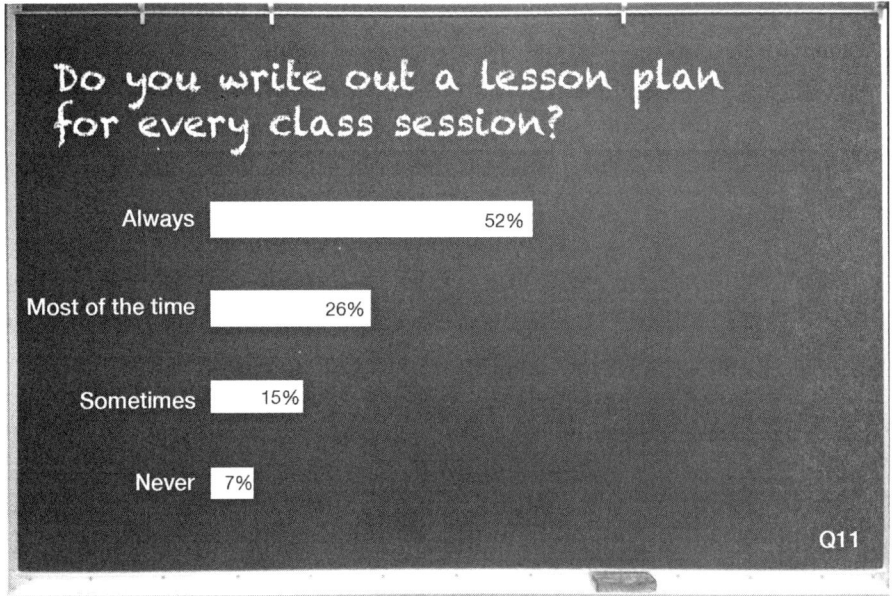

into my career, that at the beginning of a semester, when teaching a new prep, or even if I'm just pressed for time and need to achieve a certain goal before a deadline, I often jot estimated times for each part of the class in the margins of my plan.

Having a lesson written out has several advantages. First, it makes you look and feel prepared. Students notice this! If you have a written plan, you can write a short agenda on the board and give a little introduction at the beginning of the class. I write a brief agenda because I like to let students know something fun or engaging is coming that day, or that if they don't like the first few activities there may be something they like later on.

One caveat about sharing your agenda with the students: If you tend to over-prepare, be careful about being too detailed with what you put on the board. Case in point: Many years ago I took an Italian class on Saturday mornings through a continuing education program. Each morning, the teacher wrote a long plan on the board and the AV department rolled an overhead projector into the room. (Yes, this was a long time ago!) Each day we got through perhaps two or three items on the teacher's long agenda before she got stuck in what I liked to call "teacher story time." We never used that overhead! This experience made such a significant impression on me that I always change the agenda on the board if we get off track so that students see that I am aware that we got off track.

> "**If I don't write it down**, how will I remember what I did and how I did it? I find the better the written plan—especially when I make corrections to how it actually ended up happening—the better it is for me when I teach a similar point later in the semester or in another semester."
>
> *Georgia Mae Oates*

Another advantage of writing out lessons is that it gives a record to look back on. Carol Ischinger writes, "After each class, I spend time evaluating what I did, what worked and what didn't, and what I need to do next." I keep my lesson plans in spiral notebooks and amend the plans as I go. That is, if I over-plan and do not get through everything, I cross that part out and move it to the next day or week. This makes it easy to look back when I teach the same course again or if I want to share my plans with a new teacher.

As conscientious as I am about writing my plans, I often don't even look at them once I get to class. I do sometimes make a show of consulting my notebook—as if to say to the students, "I know you had to prepare for this class; look, I did too." But I find once I write the plan down it usually stays in my head. It's like writing a grocery list and not having to consult it once I'm in the supermarket.

> "**I may not refer** to the written plan during the class, but the process of writing out the lesson helps me think through how I will use the class time."
>
> *Jane Stanga*

Teachers report one major guiding principle when writing out their lesson plans—whether they write a short list or a more elaborate plan—and that is the need to be flexible. First, many teachers plan for ways to extend their lessons if their main plan doesn't last the whole class. Brian Anthon points out that students "expect and deserve well-prepared lessons. I've even learned to over-plan and always have extension materials and activities with me for when things go more quickly than anticipated."

Flexibility is not just about extension materials. Over and over in my survey, teachers wrote about the need to write a plan but to be open to changing the plan once the class begins. Some activities go faster than you might expect; some need to be slowed down or need some supplement or repetition. Sometimes a teachable moment pops up that cannot be ignored! Agnes Malicka reports that she builds into her plans "a lot of room for spontaneous learning situations." And Jim Toepper notes, "Flexibility and listening to students is an essential quality of good instruction."

> **Claire Cirolia makes** a slightly different point about teaching based on assessment—planning for time to go over assessments: "I always leave time to review our quizzes and tests when I return them to the students. It may sound obvious, but I use them as teaching tools to instruct and help students learn from their errors."

Another point to keep in mind when planning lessons is that they should be driven not only by your syllabus but also by frequent assessment. Many of us use the same textbooks and supplemental materials over and over, but no class period is ever exactly the same from one semester to the next. This is because we teach the students, not the subject. Albert VanLanduyt puts it this way: "I've been teaching my courses for seven years straight and am well-prepared, which allows me to focus on the students and their particular issues with the material being taught." By using fairly constant assessment (written and oral quizzes, homework, summaries, short and longer writings), we can achieve a flow from day to day and week to week in our planning. This means that we need to be ready, from one class to the next or even within one class, to change the direction of our plan. I generally have my lesson plan notebook open while I'm grading assignments. I jot down notes about what my students are struggling with and issues that I need to address, and then I can plan my next few classes based on that.

This flexibility is essential. A trap we don't want to fall into is over-planning and then being determined, at all costs, to make it through the plan. Of course, over-planning to ensure that you have some extension materials on hand is one thing, but novice teachers may fall into the over-planning trap.

When we hire teachers or conduct teacher-training programs, we don't really set out clear guidelines on how much time should be spent on planning. We do generally say that teachers should expect to spend one hour prepping and grading for each hour of class time, but the truth is that some novice teachers may spend hours crafting the perfect lesson plan. Then they may feel committed to getting everything on the plan done in one class, which can lead to the dreaded "coverage"—covering pages of a textbook or a list of grammar points without really engaging students in the learning. Over-planning, as well as over-grading, can lead to teacher burnout as well. One antidote to over-planning is to create a weekly plan rather than a daily one to avoid rushing through an extensive plan in one class session.

> "New teachers should realize that they should not be a slave to a lesson plan. The plan is a tool for them to use while they are actively teaching a concept."
>
> Elaine George

Sometimes when I teach a new prep, I am guilty of over-planning. I spend a couple of hours planning a two-hour class (not counting time needed for grading), and then I sort of pre-teach the class in my head on the drive to school. When I actually get into the class, I feel I've lost the spark that I need to create something that feels organic and spontaneous. I once heard that a good plan for a piece of writing is like a map that you consult before you visit a city. It gives you a general idea about the city, but you won't really know what the city is like until you are standing on the street looking around. I think a lesson plan can be the same—a general framework onto which we layer sights and sounds after the class begins. As Claire Cirolia puts it, "We've all learned that lesson plans are just that—plans—and that we have to be prepared for different things to come up in class."

Lesson Plan Templates

Teacher-training programs often teach a lesson-plan format that may look like this:

- ❏ A warm-up or hook to get students into the topic of the class. This may also include a review of a previous lesson or topic.
- ❏ Explanation or presentation of new material. This is often teacher-led.
- ❏ Controlled practice with a focus on accuracy.
- ❏ Communicative or open-ended practice.
- ❏ Application of the new skill, evaluation of whether students "got it," and feedback from students.

Teachers report being familiar with this format for planning lessons but not using it all the time (see Figure 5).

> "**It's good for the students** to have an expectation of how the class will be conducted. This helps cut down on confusion. If I vary much from my usual routine, I write the lesson format on the board at the beginning of class."
>
> *Judy Snyder*

Figure 5

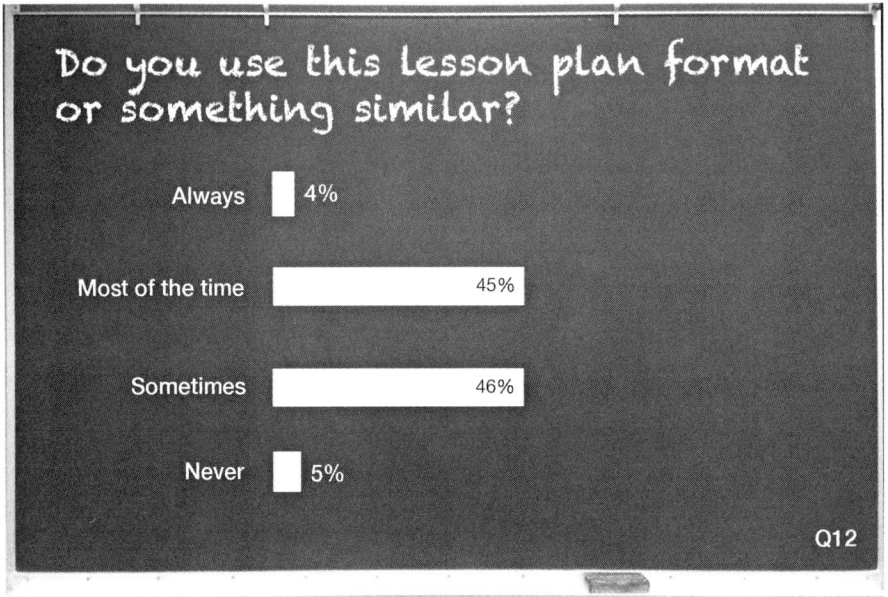

There are advantages to using such a format. For new teachers, it helps guard against too much teacher talk, moving students into practice and evaluation as a matter of routine. In addition, many teachers report using a lesson plan format at the beginning of the semester more than later on. Such a routine helps students get into the rhythm of the class, and students like knowing what to expect. Teachers also point out that the progression in this format is quite intuitive; perhaps we don't overtly think we are planning lessons in this format, but we generally move through these steps over and over, using the elements as the building blocks of the lessons.

That said, if we were to adhere to this format with little reflection, our classes might seem quite repetitive and even stilted. I had the chance to visit several classes in an EFL environment several years ago. In each class the teacher seemed to move lockstep through the first four steps of this format, often with little connection or logical flow. After witnessing several such classes and puzzling over why each class seemed to be the same mostly unconnected series of activities, I asked the program director about this. I learned that the teachers had been taught this template and were required to use it. I understood their struggle in putting novice teachers and volunteers in the classroom, but the flow of the class was definitely an issue. As Lisa Stelle points out, "I think it is great to have a plan to follow if you aren't sure what to do in your classroom, but I don't believe this format has to be followed exactly the same way each time you are in the classroom. The needs of the class and the goals that have to be accomplished change each day, so it's important to remain flexible."

> "It's not always practical to follow all these steps in all lessons. Sometimes a lesson plan will be mostly presentation of new material or mostly practice. It just depends on the concept that I'm trying to teach."
>
> *Leslie Sheen*

In commenting on the value of the lesson plan template, several teachers pointed out the importance of the first step: the warm-up, hook, or review. I find myself guilty of launching straight into presenting new information in my classes. I've been thinking about the class non-stop for hours, after all, and I forget that my students might not have been doing the same. As Janice Hornyak points out, "The warm-up/review/hook time is important to me because students are busy and are coming from other classes. They need a chance to remember what we are doing and get into it."

> **Peter Ruffner writes**, "A lot of teachers don't know how valuable Step 1 is. For one thing, students need to understand the value of what they're being taught before going through the other steps."

While teachers are generally in favor of this lesson plan format or template for organizing some lessons, this is not to say they work through the five steps in every class session. In longer classes, the pattern may be repeated several times over in one class meeting. In classes that meet frequently, the first class of the week may contain the first two steps, and the next class or classes may begin with a review/warm-up and contain a variety of practices. The format may be more useful in a grammar-based curriculum but does lend itself to other skills. It may also be more useful in a situation in which much of the work of the course is done in class or when the makeup of the class varies a lot from one class meeting to the next, as in some adult education programs with flexible attendance policies, as opposed to a "flipped" class or a class that requires extensive homework.

> **Cathleen McCargo says** this about using and adapting this template: "Depending on the lesson, there may be class sessions when the entire time may be devoted to the 'application' piece, especially if the students have completed a unit and are doing some type of performance-based assessment to evaluate their overall learning."

In addition to shifting elements depending on where the class is within a unit of instruction, other teachers shift elements because they want their students to engage in task-based learning. Megan Calvert explains this: "I like to warm up/activate schema, do a little planning and preparation for a task, do the task, and then reflect on it and work on accuracy as needed." She notes that this puts communication first, stressing that "accuracy is just a part of getting to effective communication (being more or less important depending on the context). It fits with my own learning style, which is that I like to dive in and try without feeling like I have to get it right the first time."

Besides moving toward task-based learning, many teachers are in a position to ask students to do more outside of class using technology. If you "flip" your classroom, then the hook moves to the end of the class time to give students motivation and context for what they are to view or read before the next class meeting.

Finally, if you direct your students to high-quality online grammar exercises and flash cards, you can adjust the controlled practice portion of class time and move that to homework. In any case, as we rely more on task-based activities or technology, the building blocks of good planning will most likely continue to be in play, just in a different order and in different proportions.

Flipping the ESL Classroom

As was mentioned in the Preface, this work is a snapshot in time. This means that while much of what is written here are tried-and-true methods and techniques, some of our thinking about best practices is evolving. One concept that fits in this category is the notion of a flipped lesson plan, or a flipped classroom. Briefly, in a flipped classroom, traditional classroom activities such as direct instruction become at-home activities, and activities that are traditionally done for homework, including textbook exercises, reading, and writing, are moved to class time. Thus, in a traditional classroom students may learn about something in class (say, when to use passive voice, how to pronounce –ed endings, how to annotate text, or what a good persuasive essay looks like), and then they are asked to apply those skills at home by completing exercises, reading and marking text, or drafting an essay. In a flipped classroom, students study how to use passive voice, how to pronounce –ed endings, how to annotate text, and what a good persuasive essay looks like **at home,** and then they are asked to complete the exercises, mark some text, or draft the essay **in class**—while the teacher is available for support.

> **Robyn Brinks Lockwood writes** about how she adjusts the flow of her lessons by using out-of-class assignments: "I am flipping the classroom more and more, so I skip Step 2 (explanation or presentation of new material) most of the time because they've done that outside of class. Sometimes Step 3 (controlled practice with a focus on accuracy) is also done out of class, so I focus more on Steps 4 and 5 (communicative, open-ended practice and application/evaluation) and plan more activities in my lesson."

Teachers who flip their lessons say that this has made their classrooms more social and cooperative. They claim that the technique accommodates students who work at different paces, and they like that they have moved from being "the sage on the stage" to "the guide on the side." Robyn Brinks Lockwood notes, "I get much, much better results when students work in class."

Many teachers claim that flipped instruction is blended learning at its best—better than hybrid classes in which classes meet "live" for 50 percent of the time, usually one class session per week, and are online for the other half of the allotted time. They feel that flipped teaching integrates technology seamlessly into instruction. However, it's also very feasible to flip a classroom without relying on technology if students work with textbooks and scaffolded handouts at home.

> **"Flipping has two dimensions.** It is about taking what used to be homework and doing it in class, and taking what used to be classwork and making it homework. It's also about flipping Bloom's taxonomy. Usually we make sure students comprehend in class and then we send them out to (or hope that they'll eventually be able to) synthesize, analyze, evaluate. Flipping has the students manage the 'easier' comprehension on their own. Then in class they engage in activities to actually apply the content and use the higher-order thinking skills."
>
> *Robyn Brinks Lockwood*

I have recently had several conversations and email exchanges with colleagues who are interested in learning more about flipping their classrooms, and there was quite a bit of interest in this issue at TESOL 2014.

Teachers who haven't tried flipping their classes have several questions and reservations about the practice. First, a common example of a flipped lesson is this: Instead of showing a video clip in class, assign it for homework. Give students a link to a YouTube video, and they can watch it as many times as they want and even show it to their family. Teachers who are new to flipping say that sounds great, but that they teach more than oral communication. They are eager for more examples of flipped lesson plans.

Then teachers who flip give a few more examples. In a composition class, students study the organization of an essay and read some samples on their own before coming to class. In a grammar class, students view videos or podcasts—either found on the Internet or created by the teacher, or they study charts and examples. The skeptical teacher says, isn't that what my students do already for homework?

There is indeed a difference between assigning homework and flipping a class. First, a flipped classroom really violates students' expectations of how the class is supposed to work. Therefore, teachers who flip need to be very deliberate about the practice. In my non-flipped class, I may suggest to my composition students that they read the explanation in the textbook of, say, how to write a conclusion and to study the samples in the book before coming to class. But I progress with my lesson plan as if only some of the students have done this homework, becoming the "sage on the stage" during class time.

> **Robyn Brinks Lockwood writes** about how she flips her lesson on research paper introductions: In a traditional class, "students understand the components and can recognize them in the samples. However, when they get home to write their own introductions, it's a challenge. They can't seem to apply what we studied to their papers. Since I've flipped the classroom, we do the actual writing in class. I move about the room being the 'guide on the side,' and help students on a more individual basis. The drafts are due at the end of class and they're usually much stronger than what I'd receive when they do it on their own. Students also like this."

In a flipped class, it needs to be made very clear to students that what I traditionally think of as "preview for the next class" homework is actually the most important—or only—homework. Then the skeptical teacher asks, "What about my students who don't do this prep? How am I going to conduct the class if only half of my students have engaged in the homework to learn about passive voice or past tense endings?" Teachers who flip will respond with techniques to ensure students are engaging with content at home. For example, they have students fill in scaffolded notes sheets—either paper or in electronic form—as they view lessons, with instructions to copy notes and specific examples, and to answer questions. Then they give students quizzes at the beginning of class to hold students accountable and to discover what is still not clear. They say that once students know you are serious about having them engage in lessons outside of class, they rise to the occasion.

Teachers who flip their classrooms say that they often construct their lessons following a three-stage lesson: Explore, Flip, Apply. They explore in class (the hook), flip direct instruction to homework, and in the following class, students apply what they have learned. To illustrate, I can flip the first two days of my persuasive essay unit in this fashion. On Day One, I have my students explore moral dilemmas. I give them scenarios to discuss in groups. Each group gets a different dilemma (e.g., you find a bag containing $10,000 that you know was hidden by drug dealers; you find a copy of an upcoming test in the restroom; your irresponsible friend asks you to write a letter of recommendation for a job at your workplace). Each group decides on their solution and presents both the dilemma and their solution to the class. Then the class period ends with some group brainstorming: What makes a good argument? Students will most likely come up with good ideas on the topic. They'll brainstorm the need to support with facts and not emotion and the need to examine both sides of the argument.

At that point, students are ready to go home and study. They view a PowerPoint that I have created that spells out the essential pieces of a persuasive essay, from types of introductions and what the thesis might look like to how to construct a counterargument and refutation. The PowerPoint also contains several possible topics for the students to consider.

In the next class, as students walk in the room, they take a quiz, which I collect. This quiz will tell me very quickly who didn't do the homework, and I have the option of asking those students to leave, go to a lab on campus, and view the PowerPoint. After the quiz, I have group time in which the same quiz is discussed, and I allow time for questions. In my two-hour class, I now have at least an hour left for students to choose a topic, create an outline, and start to write. I usually sit down at the teacher's desk or at a desk or table in the middle of the group and quietly confer with the students as they write.

As this example shows, the part of the lesson in which students are usually quietly taking notes has been moved to homework time, and the work that needs higher-order thinking is done while I am present to answer questions. This plan accommodates students who work at different paces. They can view the PowerPoint as many times as necessary at home, clicking through as quickly or slowly as they need to. And after they begin drafting in class, they can finish writing at home at their own pace.

In essence, flipped classrooms contain the same lesson plan elements as a traditional classroom but take advantage of the "information age." As we become used to having information at our fingertips around the clock, we are able to move some instruction out of the classroom to make the classroom experience more student-centered with more student engagement.

Lesson planning for ESL classes takes into account our unique challenges. We teach a skill and not information, so we have to be careful to craft plans that move our students forward in their acquisition and be mindful not to simply cover material or pages in a text. We are usually faced with bringing together students from many cultures and first languages and from many educational systems and we then write plans that take that into account. We generally know the building blocks of a good plan—something that includes some teacher-led instruction, some practice, and some application—and we experiment with the order of those building blocks as we try to make our classrooms communicative or task-based, inductive or deductive, and as we consider flipping instruction and otherwise integrating technology into our teaching.

Chapter 4
Bringing Variety to Lesson Plans

While it may be easy to view class planning as filling in the blanks in a progression from warm up to presentation to practice and assessment, there are many other factors that teachers keep in mind when planning their lessons. This chapter deals with those factors as well as adjusting for different paces and spicing lessons up with activities and games.

Guiding Principles

The first principle that many teachers follow is to connect what they are teaching to their students' worlds. This may include linking new concepts to students' background knowledge, using students' names, current issues affecting your school, and students' experiences in your examples, and generally making the class experience relevant and engaging. As Vivian Leskes points out, "Of maximum importance is giving students material that is engaging." In addition to creating plans that are relevant and engaging, Mike J. Waguespack maintains that lessons should "require or encourage students to use critical-thinking skills to process information, and not just 'parrot' what they have read, heard, and/or seen."

> "One of the principles I try to keep in mind is relevance. I want students to understand why the lesson is important."
>
> Kathleen Wax

Recently I felt that my teaching was getting stale, so I made myself a simple promise: No matter what the title of the course, I would be sure my plan would allow each learner to use all four skills—listening, speaking, reading, and writing—plus include some explicit, direct instruction in either grammar/language or vocabulary. I also try to keep in mind to pre-teach any vocabulary needed for a task or assignment, no matter what the skill area of the course. This means that my oral communication students learn words like *volume, rate,* and *stress*; my reading students learn *heading, caption,* and *transition*; my composition students learn *lead, unity,* and *coherence*; and so on.

> Judy Snyder explains one point she keeps in mind when she is planning her lessons: "Use class time efficiently. It's amazing how fast time can disappear, especially if you haven't given some thought as to how long an explanation or activity is likely to take."

And, finally, I try not to forget to tell students **why** we are doing what we are doing. I know that the purpose for discussing journals related to our novel is that having an affective or emotional response (rather than just an efferent—information-finding—response) improves reading ability, and I think it helps students to hear that. I believe that editing papers with minimal written input from me helps students become stronger writers, and I have to remember to tell students that when they expect me to mark or fix every error. I know that learners create new neural pathways when they memorize vocabulary until it is automatic, and I stress that in my classes. I believe that my students come to me to learn but also to learn how to learn, so I try to remember to include these points in my lesson plans. I think, or at least hope, that by explaining the reasons we spend class time on different activities I can avoid having students just "go through the motions" and instead engage purposefully in what we are doing.

Many teachers report keeping in mind the need for a variety of activities and interactions, with a balance of teacher talk versus student talk, a balance of teacher-led versus pair and group work, and so on. They note that they look for strategies that keep teacher talk to a minimum. Darlene Branges adds, "Keep the pacing crisp, so activities flow from one to the next." Lesson plans are often written in manageable chunks of 20 minutes or so. Chunks that are much longer, especially in a lower-level, tax students' ability to absorb. Boring or dry activities can be scheduled early in the class before students get too tired.

> **Kay Marshall reports** on her thought process as she plans her lessons: "What are the big skills students HAVE TO master by the end of the unit (e.g., how to use a certain verb tense or how to organize a compare-contrast paragraph)? How can I vary the types of activities throughout the class to keep them interested (e.g., direct instruction, pair/group activities, individual seatwork, collective classwork led by students at the board)? How can I assess if they've learned what we set out to learn (e.g., quiz, homework assignment, random checks, circulating)?"

Many teachers like to plan opportunities for their students to move during the class time, and they plan opportunities for quiet time as well. As Gregory Kennerly writes, "One of my guiding principles is to give the learners enough time to process any information I give them. I do not find moments of silence in the classroom awkward." And Suzanne Mele Szwarcewicz likes to incorporate think-pair-share often. She writes, "When possible, I have students do some personal think time (usually brief), and then some sharing."

> **"Each class needs quiet** writing time, up-and-about moving around time, and talking-quietly-with-a-partner time. And of course teacher-talking time."
>
> *Elizabeth O'Brien*

While teachers report the importance of using a variety of modes and interactions in the classroom, it is easy to take this to an extreme. Students appreciate a mix of activities within a class hour or session, but that does not mean they show up each day expecting a different set of activities from the days or weeks before. In language classes, repetition is your friend. It's especially important that we establish patterns for the beginning and the end of class. Patterns for how work is turned in or how homework is assigned can save a lot of time—both in your lesson planning and in the class, and this is time that can be used more productively.

In my classes, I always write (brief) directions on the board, and this is a pattern that my students come to expect. Another useful pattern is one that signals the class is about to end. This can help avoid the premature "packing up" that I sometimes notice. It takes classes as much as 6 to 8 class sessions to learn a routine—remember, it's new to them even if you've been doing it for years—so it's best to be patient while the students learn your patterns.

As human beings, we like patterns and routines, but that doesn't mean our teaching needs to be dull or overly repetitive. I generally like to change up my teaching strategies from one semester to another so that I don't get bored with my teaching, but within a semester I normally set up a certain number of kinds of activities and repeat each several or even many times. I want my students to know that if they are using an anticipation guide, discussing journals, putting a sample composition in order, or checking homework with the document camera, they'll do the activity **the same way** each time we do it. Bill Woodard explains this well: "One principle that I stick to in planning all of my classes is to make them as regular as possible. That is, I want students to know what to expect in each class. Similarly, another principle that I adhere to is to not test students using completely different tasks than those they have been practicing in class and at home."

> "Repetition is an important part of learning, so recycling activities into subsequent lessons is helpful."
>
> *Cathleen McCargo*

Another point to keep in mind when you are planning lessons is how to schedule work that is going to take a lot of your time to grade. You don't want to give a big summarizing test in your reading class, an in-class essay in your writing class, and film student speeches in your oral communication class all in the same week. You have to strike a balance between assessing when students are ready and when you have time to grade the assessments. In my program, we strive to give very prompt feedback. What that means for me is sometimes it works better to delay an assessment a week to have time to get to it promptly. Other ways to cut down on grading time include having group assignments with group grades and using rubrics to grade assignments. It's important to consider the time needed for grading while you plan, as you'll want to set up the group assignments in your plan or introduce and explain the grading rubric when you give the assignment. These strategies take a little up-front time, but are well worth it when grading time comes.

A final point that teachers keep in mind while planning their classes is the importance of scaffolding. We teach a limited number of courses in my program, so I wind up teaching the same classes again and again. I always remember the students' final products but don't always remember the road that got us there. In other words, sometimes I forget the struggle that it took to accomplish a task, and therefore I am guilty of rushing through the process at times. Successful teachers understand the enabling skills that students need to accomplish a larger task, and spending time on those enabling skills is valuable scaffolding time. Elisabeth Chan stresses the importance of this: "Model and scaffold! Whatever the assignment or activity is, don't cut out or slack in the modeling and scaffolding. It's really important for the students to better understand what you are asking them to do."

Scaffolding means that in my lower-level class I spend time on the pronunciation of the –s ending on present verbs before we start an activity that involves speaking in present tense. In my intermediate composition class, we brainstorm how to create maps with supporting ideas over and over. I model it first on the board, and then groups work on maps that they share on the document camera. In my upper-level composition class, students memorize transition signals for their persuasive essay so those phrases come to them automatically when they write their exit essay test. This means that while I am planning my classes, I have the goal in mind but have to think of ways to model and practice the enabling skills that get the students to that goal.

Planning for Different Paces

Issues including everything from personality to age to language background and preferred learning style contribute to the fact that our students work at different paces. In classes in which students are expected to engage in a variety of activities and create products, difference in the speed which students work must be accommodated. Teachers have a lot of tips on how to make this happen.

> **Robyn Brinks Lockwood notes** that students who work at different paces were more of a problem in the past, but "flipping my classroom has really helped with this." Students work at their own pace both at home and in class.

In some cases, as when students take tests or write essays in class, teachers schedule assignments for the end of a class or before a break so that the slower workers don't feel pressured. Faster students leave the room or pull out a book or phone/tablet when finished. That is not to say that students should have an unlimited amount of time for a task; language often needs to be spontaneous and automatic. Recently I've been giving short vocabulary quizzes that some students finish in five minutes while others seem to need fifteen minutes or more. In those cases, I've been timing the students, and I announce that the slowest students get no more than double the time the fastest took. The result is that the students who are slower on the first quiz realize that they need to spend more time memorizing the vocabulary so that their knowledge becomes automatic. By the end of the semester, the slower students usually take only slightly longer than the fastest.

Sometimes work expands to fill the time you give it, so I like to be clear about how much time I think students should spend on an activity and note this in my plan. For example, when my students are working alone or in pairs, I usually tell them how long they will be working and write this on the board. I shave a few minutes off of what I really think the activity will take to motivate the slower students to get to work. Then, when the time is up and they aren't finished, I negotiate an extension. Once our final time is determined, I give a two-minute warning, and then usually a "finish the sentence you are working on" warning, and then time is up.

Many teachers report using group work to even out differences in pacing. Sometimes faster students can be grouped together while the teacher spends time with the slower students. The faster groups can be given a longer or more challenging task. Also, if the groups are completing exercises, Karen Van Horn suggests that "the faster students come and write the answers on the board while the slower students are still working. By the time the answers are on the board, the slower students are generally ready and we can discuss as a class."

Besides this tip, many teachers bring extension activities for the faster groups to continue working on while the slower groups complete the main task. I often write a list of tasks to be completed on the board, with the last being optional or open-ended. This works to keep the class humming, and the slower students don't even realize that the faster ones are two tasks ahead of them.

Teachers also even out pacing by grouping faster and slower students together. If I am pressed for time, I assign the faster writer to be the "recorder" of the group.

> "Typically, students do group work that allows them to work with those students with similar skills and who work at a similar pace. Then I'll switch groups to have students work with those whose skills are quite different and whose pace is different as well."
>
> *Cheri Bridgeforth*

For individual work that is not a test or quiz, it's a good idea to watch the students work. As the faster students finish, you can give a few warnings and then ask everyone who is not finished to complete the task for homework. The quick finishers might need to be counseled to slow down, as well. As Marilyn Odaka points out, "Some students finish quickly because they rush through the exercise, so I encourage them to double check their work. In many cases, I tell students who finish early to find a classmate who has also finished and cross-check their answers."

Finally, I always tell my students that their homework time is the time for them to work at the pace that is exactly right for them. I insist on doing or at least starting a lot of work in class. I believe this time on task shows students what a reasonable amount of time is. Those students who race through a draft of a composition at home in 20 minutes may realize that a composition drafted in an hour is much better. And on the other side of a coin, a student who suffers over a draft of a composition for four hours over two days can see that a draft produced in an hour can be quite good. That said, it still may take some students twice as long as others to do a good job on homework, so I usually build that into my assignments. I'll say at the beginning of the semester, "You should plan on spending seven to ten hours a week on homework for this class. If you are spending much more or much less than that, please let me know."

> "I try to give a combination of in-class and out-of-class assignments so that the students who need more time can take it at home."
>
> Rebecca Wolff

Activities and Games in the Classroom

Many ESL teachers like to use a variety of activities and games in their classes. A quick Google search for Find Someone Who ESL activity yielded hundreds of thousands of hits. We play charades, 20 questions, Concentration, Jeopardy!, Two Truths and a Lie. We tape names on our students' backs to play Who am I? We bring in board games like Scrabble or Boggle and board games that we make ourselves. We play Hangman, we play Bingo, and we do crossword puzzles. We have groups choose who gets the heart transplant. We have groups discuss moral dilemmas and form human Likert scales. Students participate in role plays and in reader's theater. Even peer review of writing can be seen as an activity that must be learned. All of these require that students understand the learning purpose of the game or activity, learn how to play or participate, and use the appropriate language structures.

> "I've had some students who love games and take to them quickly. Other times I've had groups that didn't really like games or who took a long time to learn them. If the group seems to like games and learn them quickly, I am more apt to use them more frequently."
>
> Leslie Sheen

Given the amount and variety of games out there—and the fact that they are even built in to some of our textbooks—how and how often we use such activities needs to be considered.

Teachers understand that it takes valuable class time to introduce a new activity. Thus, most teachers introduce a new kind of activity just a few times a semester (see Figure 6).

I am usually very deliberate about tying the game or activity to my teaching objective. In a grammar class, I may say, "We have seen that present perfect is used to talk about actions that occurred recently, at an unspecified time. A great way to get lots of practice with that is this Find Someone Who activity." Or in a lower level, I might say, "We have been working hard on yes-no questions. Now we have a game called Twenty Questions, and the interesting thing about this game is that only yes-no questions are allowed, so let's play." Using Two Truths and a Lie is a great way to get across the concept of using *used to* for something that the speaker did habitually in the past but doesn't do anymore. Thus, in my class the choice of fun activity is usually driven by the grammar point we are covering, and not vice versa.

In a composition class, I tell my classes that good writing has unity and coherence—words and phrases that work like glue to hold the piece

Figure 6

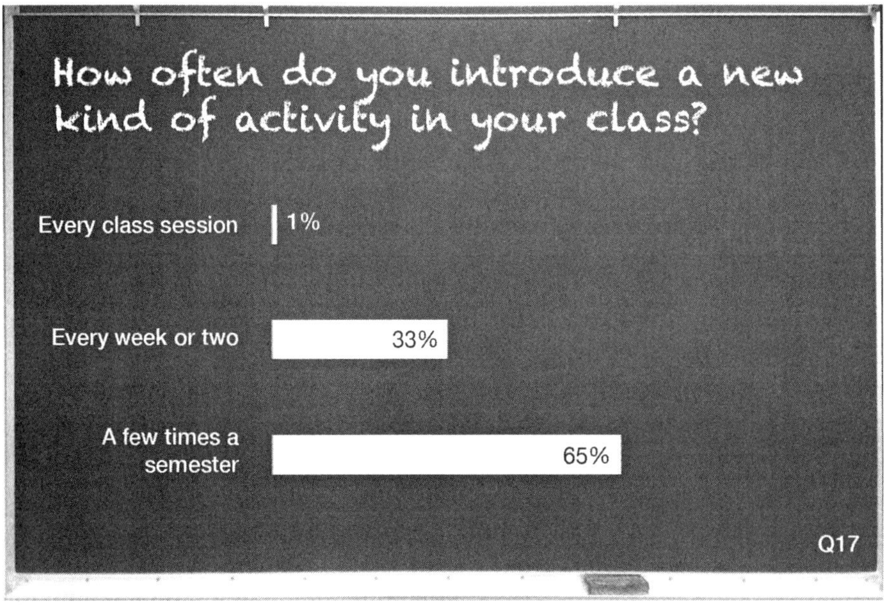

How often do you introduce a new kind of activity in your class?

Every class session	1%
Every week or two	33%
A few times a semester	65%

Q17

Note: Additional responses to this item appear in Appendix 3.

4 Bringing Variety to Lesson Plans   51

Figure 7

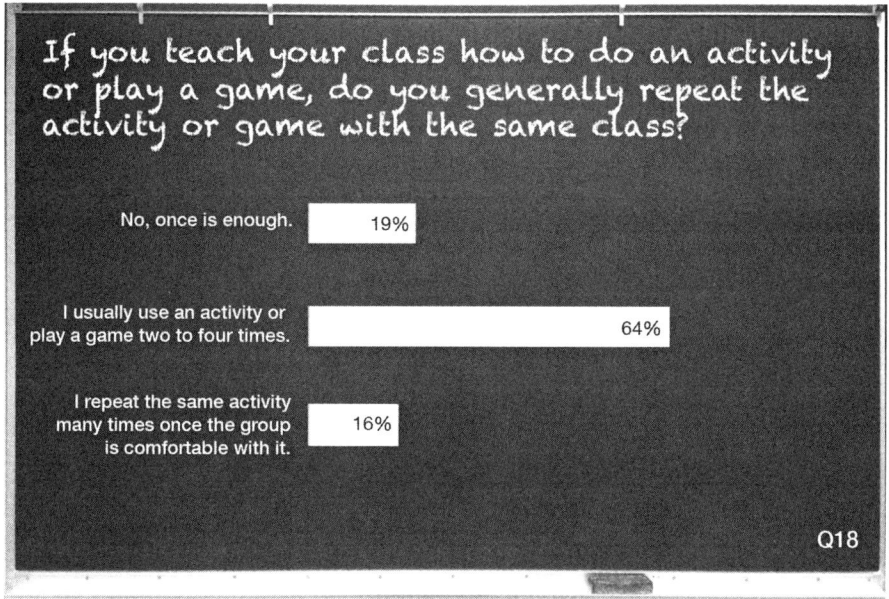

together. A great way to illustrate this is to cut up a composition and ask students to piece it back together using the signal phrases as clues. This kinesthetic exercise can be fun and groups can compete to see who finishes first, but above all the focus is on the learning. In my opinion, rather than being a supplement to what is in my textbook, this fun activity is actually the best way to convey my point, but I need to be deliberate about that. I don't say, for example, "Class, you've been working very hard, so now let's have some fun." Instead, I say, "I believe the activity we are about to do is the best way to help you learn how unity and coherence hold an essay together."

Teachers know that learning a new language, especially as an adult, is hard work, and they want to bring some fun into the classroom. But at the same time, students can't see our classes as "fun time." Teachers use activities as supplements, to add spice, or to motivate students. And once they invest the time in teaching students how to do an activity, teachers generally repeat it a few times as long as the activity is integrated into the lesson and helps students learn the material (see Figure 7). Teachers know that they need to find a balance when there are limited contact hours; activities have to move the class toward our goal. As Wendy Asplin writes, "*Games* is a term that might sound like it's just about fun. Of course it's about fun, but the important thing is that it really does use the structure we're working on. Otherwise, it's not a good use of time, except perhaps on a weary Friday or a joyful end of the quarter."

> **Megan Calvert reports** on her motivation for introducing something new: "I introduce new games or activities either when we need inspiration (myself included), or when I have a fun idea and have the time to flesh it out. Sometimes a creative mood just strikes me—it might not be part of a well-planned strategy, but it's an important part of my own sanity and enjoyment as a teacher to try new things and use my creativity."

Influences from Our L2 Experiences

Many teachers report that their teaching has been molded by their experiences learning a second or third language and that often shows in their approach to lesson planning. I often say that I became an ESL teacher because I knew there was a better way to teach than I'd been taught. I couldn't teach a foreign language because, well, I'd never learned one well enough. So English it was. And I do feel so much more successful in what I do than my teachers were with me. I believe that I am not a good language learner, and I feel that has made me more empathetic to my students and has made me search for and employ a wide variety of approaches to engage all kinds of learners.

> **DeAnna Coon reflects** on how her foreign language classes have shaped her teaching: "I remember a lot of text-based learning, rote memorization, etc., in my language classes. Sometimes I design activities in ways that I remember being helpful to me, but, in general, I don't approach my classes in the same way my teachers did. Of course, they were just teaching language; I don't remember a lot of content integration, which is a greater focus for me."

4 Bringing Variety to Lesson Plans

Teachers report that they empathize with students and make choices about their teaching because they've experienced what it's like to learn a second language. Judy Snyder writes, "If I could require that every ESL teacher must have had experience in learning at least one foreign language, I would do so. There's no way to fully empathize with and understand a student who is struggling to learn a new language if you haven't been through it yourself." And Elisabeth Chan notes, "I know it's easy to say, 'I studied a foreign language, so I understand what my students are going through,' but I think that has to show and be apparent in your class and to your students." She advises, "Bring in specific stories of your own experiences with language learning and what was tough about it. Think about your struggles when you plan lessons, and think about what would've been helpful for you."

> **Mike J. Waguespack** writes about how his experiences learning French guide his lesson planning: "One of my standard checks of reasonableness of an assignment or activity is for me to try to do it myself in my second language (French), and to see how much (or little) I struggle. This helps me to either avoid 'frustrational' assignments, or at least to plan on providing the necessary support so that students can handle them."

Of course, our teaching styles are shaped by all of our learning (and life) experiences. I frequently remember how frustrated I was as a member of a large, and very good, chorale. Our conductor would often stop us and say, "That wasn't right; try again." That instruction was completely wasted on me. When she would say instead, "That was good; do it that way again," then I would perk up and learn. Mary Charleza also reports on being shaped by learning music: "When I take a music lesson and return thinking that I've practiced correctly only to find that I focused on the wrong thing, I'm mad at myself but am also taking mental notes on my students who sometimes don't 'get it' even though they thought they understood too! That's why I like to practice skills over several classes. You never know how much has really been 'gotten,' how much is wanting class to be over, and how much is good guessing!"

Teachers may seem calm and relaxed when they enter their classroom and unpack their book bags, pulling out their textbooks, papers they've graded, quizzes, items like colored pencils or playing cards, and so on. They are calm on the surface, but below the surface are many thought processes. Indeed, well-prepared teachers come to class having thought through multiple dimensions of the class. They have planned both the content and the pacing of the class, while at the same time being open to seizing a teachable moment and changing direction. They have planned a reasonable amount of carefully chosen activities that offer variety without putting the focus on learning the activity rather than learning the language. They usually have one eye on the clock and the other on the students as they gauge when it's time to move to the next activity or ask students to finish for homework. And they always have one more extension activity or game if their plan runs short.

Chapter 5
Planning for Student Questions

In a student-centered classroom, students should feel free to ask questions. However, teachers often face issues at opposite ends of a continuum when it comes to student questions. At one end of the continuum, we have too many questions. In essence, some students try to take over the flow of instruction with questions. And at the other end of the continuum, we have a silent class in which students don't want to or can't ask questions, perhaps as a result of coming from a more passive learning situation. This chapter offers tips and strategies for incorporating and otherwise managing questions in student-centered classrooms.

Too Many Questions

In some classes, teachers note that often one student asks many questions: 72 percent of respondents noted that they consider this situation to be potentially problematic (see Figure 8). Lisa Stelle notes, "If one student dominates the discussion or asks too many questions, the other students in the classroom usually get annoyed. They start rolling their eyes and/or sighing. At this point, the questions have become a disruption." In this case, the student who is dominating doesn't seem to understand the collaborative nature of the learning environment. Suzanne Mele Szwarcewicz agrees, writing that it "can be draining on the whole class to have one person dominate the discussion or interrupt the flow of the lesson."

Often it helps to address this issue head on. First, it's a good idea to understand why the single student is asking so many questions. Robyn Brinks Lockwood suggests that it could be "an indicator that that student either needs more help or more attention that would be better served during office hours." Indeed, many of our students are unfamiliar with the concept of office hours. Using the too-many-questions scenario is the perfect way to teach everyone about office hours. I sometimes say, "You are asking a lot of great questions, and I really like that. But I need

Figure 8

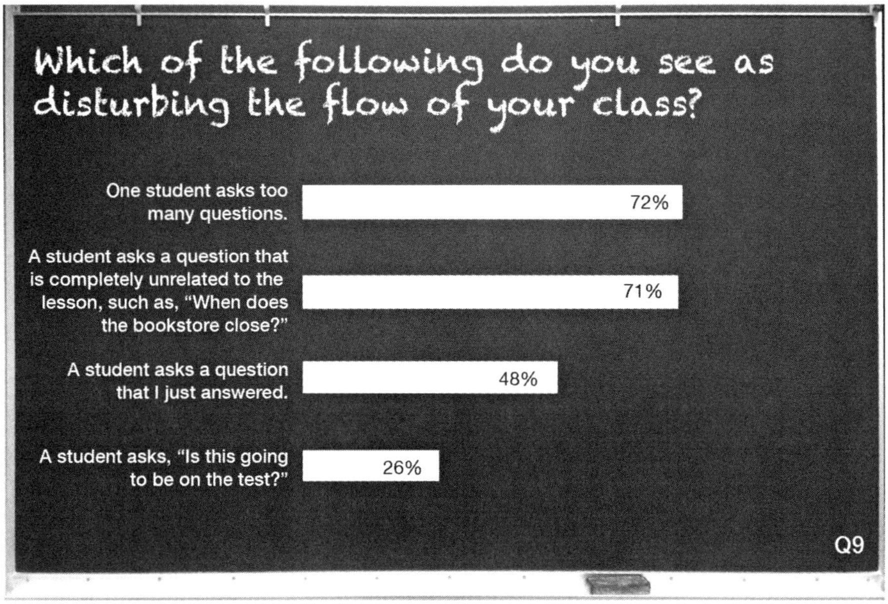

Which of the following do you see as disturbing the flow of your class?

Response	Percentage
One student asks too many questions.	72%
A student asks a question that is completely unrelated to the lesson, such as, "When does the bookstore close?"	71%
A student asks a question that I just answered.	48%
A student asks, "Is this going to be on the test?"	26%

Q9

Note: Respondents checked more than one response; totals do not add up to 100 percent. Additional responses to this item appear in Appendix 3.

you to come and sit in my office so I can be sure I have enough time to answer all of your questions fully, when I'm not thinking about the other 20 students in the class." Then, after one student does visit me in my office, I can ask that student to tell the others how useful it was to sit down and talk one-on-one in a quiet atmosphere.

Teachers also focus on having a balanced participation when it comes to asking questions in class. Allyson Noble reports that "if one

> "**Students who ask** a million questions are generally not benefiting because language is learned when it's used and practiced. It doesn't matter how many questions one asks about a topic; until he/she practices with it, it will not be completely understood. I see asking too many questions as a way of avoiding the risk of usage, and counterproductive to moving towards production."
>
> *DeAnna Coon*

5 Planning for Student Questions 57

student has a habit of asking too many questions, I usually give my students 2–3 sticky notes at the beginning of class. For each question they ask, I take one away. When they don't have any more post-its, they have to hold their questions until the end of class." I have two similar techniques. In the first, when students are editing papers that I have marked with editing symbols, I walk through the room stopping in order at each student's desk. Each time I stop, I will answer one and only one question. I usually make three or four passes through the room, following the same path, in a 30-minute editing session. My students think carefully about each question when I do this. Similarly, when students are working on a first draft of a piece of writing, I may give each student two to four index cards or pieces of colored cardstock. I sit at the teacher's desk rather than hovering over them, to give them ownership of their writing. But they may come to me for input or advice, surrendering a card on each visit.

> "I don't view any questions as problems. If they are of the type I checked (on the survey), we all laugh together and recognize them as 'off topic.' Humor is often the best antidote to class problems as long as it is not specifically directed at one student."
>
> Jane E. McGinley

Dawn Titafi encourages students to ask questions but does not let the questions take over her classes. She writes, "To maintain the flow of instruction, I usually sincerely thank the students for their great questions but hand them a blue book labeled 'Class Questions.' They can write down any questions or concerns that come up during the class period. I address them the next day as a warm-up."

Even if one student does not dominate with questions, students interrupt us all of the time with questions.

When asked if it bothers teachers when students, while working on grammar exercises, ask about the meaning of a word, not one teacher surveyed thought this would be a problem (see Q9 in Appendix 3). Indeed, Peter Ruffner points out, "It doesn't take long to answer the question and get back to the lesson. The alternative, telling the student we're not working on vocabulary right now, seems confrontational and thus counter-productive."

> "Sometimes, if a student asks too many questions, [he or she] begin[s] to dominate the class, and even if the questions are valid and topical, other students begin to feel left out or begin to rely on that student to carry the participation of the entire class. In this situation, I tend to say, 'Thank you, but you've asked (answered) a question already. Does anyone else have a question (answer)?'"
>
> *Elaine George*

Similarly, some students will interrupt a grammar explanation to ask a question about another grammar point. Only 13 percent of teachers find this disturbing or disruptive to the flow of the class (see Chart Q9 in Appendix 3). As Bill Woodard explains, "I do not consider it a problem if, when I am explaining a grammar point, a student asks about another grammar point. Grammar is interrelated and it is often difficult to isolate one point from another." Often teachers note that the question the student asks is about something they will be teaching soon—later in the same class, for example. In that case, teachers generally report not answering the student's question on the spot but promising to get to it soon—even making a note on the board of the question. When this happens in my class, I generally return to the asker of the question, saying something like, "José, this is the point you were asking about earlier, isn't it?"

In some cases, we may not have the answer to a student's question. Very few respondents (3 percent) reported that, in some cases, the answer to a question is "that's just English" (see Chart Q9 in Appendix 3). However, I have noticed that some inexperienced teachers or those who lack a background in linguistics might be inclined to give such a response. I've heard novice teachers say, "Oh, articles. Well, knowing when to use *a* and *the* is more art than science." Similarly, few teachers (6 percent) report having to respond, "I don't recall the correct rule, don't have an example of that, (etc.) and need some time to look it up" (see Chart Q9 in Appendix 3). However, I urge novice teachers to say this rather than saying "that's just English." I have needed to do this when teaching how to cite something tricky using MLA style, for example. As Gregory Kennerly notes, "I ask for time to either think or do my homework after class. I have never had students who weren't willing to be as patient with me as I am with them."

In my program, we are seeing more and more students who graduated from high school in the United States. It is these students especially who seem to ask, "Is this going to be on the test?" This question can get under the skin of some teachers: 25 percent of teachers surveyed (see Chart 8) noted that they find this question to be inappropriate. On this issue, Michele Rivera writes, "I try to express that tests only measure a fraction of knowledge, and that even if something is 'not on the test,' it is still important to learn."

Another question type is the completely off-topic question. For example, say you have just finished showing the best way to mark an article before writing a summary. You finish and ask, "Are there any questions?" Then a student asks, "What time does the bookstore close?" In a case like this, 71 percent of respondents (see Figure 8) reported that this is inappropriate and disturbs the flow of the class. It certainly takes the wind out of my sails! While most of us can turn anything into a teachable moment, it is questions like these that are most likely to lead us to lose patience. However, such a question can give some insight into whether our students are "present" in the class and engaged, or if they have lost focus or are bored. Elizabeth Rasmussen reports that she responds "by saying, 'Speak to me after class,' when I deal with both issues: not knowing how to find the bookstore hours and not following what we are doing in class."

Finally, another situation that causes teachers to lose patience is when students ask a question about something that has just been covered in the class: 50 percent of respondents (see Figure 8) noted that this is problematic. Teachers who find this irritating generally feel that students are not paying attention, are distracted, and so on. That may be the case, but the situation can be remedied. Some teachers ask the other members of the class to answer the question. This allows the other students to reiterate the information or instructions, and it reduces teacher talk. Christina Luckey notes that if the question is about instructions, she may point to what she has written on the board. She writes, "The student will 'get the picture' that it's important to focus, but also see that the instructions are reinforced in written mode."

While it's possible that students are not paying attention, it's also possible that the student who asks a question about what has just been covered simply did not understand. If this happens a lot in my classes, I generally know that I need to slow down, or more likely use more modes when I explain or give directions. I may write more on the board, use pictures or diagrams, or put a handout in front of every student.

It is interesting to note that 50 percent of respondents (see Figure 8) think that a question about something that has just been explained is problematic. That means 50 percent of respondents do not believe that is problematic. As Lori Ward notes, "I think students hear what they want to hear when they are ready to hear it, so I really don't get irritated at any question." And we really should put ourselves in our students' places. Some of our classes are very demanding, obviously in the students' second language, and we move at a pretty fast pace. Martha Wheeler writes, "I try to remember that the student may have been processing information provided earlier and may not have actually heard what I said, so I answer patiently."

Questions are truly at the heart of a learner-centered classroom. Rebecca Wolff points out that "I understand that generally students need a lot of repetition, and this is a chance for me to say something in a different way."

> "I do not usually think it is a problem if a student asks a question that I have just answered. Maybe I didn't explain it clearly, so I will try to rephrase in my answer. On the other hand, it may be a problem if the student appears to have been goofing off when I gave the explanation or instructions the first time."
>
> *Jane Stanga*

Encouraging Questions

While the past few pages have addressed the issues of too many questions or off-topic questions, often we have the opposite problem: students who are afraid to ask a question, or perhaps don't know how to ask. Isabella Strohmeyer notes, "Asking questions is how learning happens for most, so I encourage questions, not resent them."

5 Planning for Student Questions

It's good to keep in mind that, when planning lessons, we need to plan time for questions and learn how to encourage them. When I was an impressionable high school student, I worked at a fast food outlet. We were taught that, once a customer finished giving an order, we were not to ask, "Is that all?" We were told that it is human nature to want to answer yes, so we were instructed to ask instead, "And what else?" This lesson has carried over all these years in my teaching!

Keeping this tendency to want to answer yes in mind, when we finish explaining something or when students finish working on something, it's not the best strategy to ask, "Does everyone understand?" Surely most students will nod, the student who wants you to pick up the pace (perhaps to get to the break sooner!) will say yes, and so on. But just as surely, the student who doesn't understand won't speak up, either for fear of embarrassment, of slowing the class down, or because she just doesn't know what she doesn't understand yet and can't articulate a question.

A better question than "Does everyone understand?" would be, "Any questions?" But students might be reluctant to speak up even after that prompting. That's why it is even better to end an explanation with, "Someone ask me a question about this." Then, remain silent until someone does, when you can respond with, "I'm glad you asked" or "Good question" before you answer. After your answer, you can ask, "Did that answer your question?" and then say, "Next question!"

Even when you insist on questions—I sometimes say that we can only start our break after at least two students ask a question—students often have trouble explaining themselves when they have a question or doubt. For example, say I give an instruction that students are to choose three or four pages of a particular chapter of our novel and write a summary of those pages. After giving what I believe to be a pretty complete explanation, I say, "Someone ask me a question about this assignment." A student who has trouble articulating questions might ask, "What are we supposed to write?" This could be an example of what 50 percent of teachers noted as bothersome in class: students asking a question about something that was just explained (see Figure 8).

But what if the problem is that the student doesn't know how to articulate the question? What if the student really just wants to know how long the summary should be in relation to the original, or if he can choose the pages to summarize or if the teacher is choosing them, or if the summary is to be in first-person from the point of view of a character? Or perhaps I mentioned a length but that was one of a dozen details, and the student just can't remember that one detail about the assignment.

> "**If students ask questions**, it means they are listening, paying attention, and are engaged (usually!). It is up to me to manage situations that may be problematic. I often find myself saying, 'Good question!' If a student asks about something I plan to address but haven't gotten to, I will ask them to wait until I get to it, and then go back to see if I've answered the question. When needed, I say that we've got to move on, especially to the student who asks too many questions."
>
> *Claire Cirolia*

There are two ways to deal with this. The first is to simply say, "I don't really understand your question. Could you explain a little more about what you didn't understand?" And the second would be to more deliberately teach question techniques. I teach a lesson in my oral communication class on asking follow-up questions. These are in the context of asking questions after a classmate's presentation, but I know the skills will be useful in their other classes—ESL and beyond.

I teach three kinds of questions:

❏ A restatement followed by "Is this correct?" In the scenario described on page 61 and above, the student might say, "I think you said that we don't have to type our summary. Is this correct?"

❏ A request for examples. The student should repeat a little of what I said and then ask for an example or examples. In the previous scenario, the student might say, "You mentioned that we shouldn't include a lot of details in our summary. Can you give us an example of a detail from the chapter that we shouldn't include?"

❏ A request for further explanation or repetition. The student should repeat a little of what I said and then ask for further information. In the previous scenario, the student might say, "You mentioned that we should follow the same steps that we used for the last summary we wrote. Could you repeat the steps in that procedure?" Or, the student might say, "You mentioned we should avoid using direct quotes in our summary. Could you explain what that means?"

Of course, our students won't be this articulate, but with some modeling and practice they get pretty good at it, and they gain some confidence to speak up. In my scaffolded lesson, I usually ask students to study some sample questions and identify which category they fall into. Then I give a short lecture that is rather vague and that has missing information, and each student has to ask a question. I give them time to formulate the correct construction: a restatement followed by a question. We then have a few more open-ended chances for practice over the next several weeks.

Teachers need to guide the flow of a student-centered class, and managing questions from students is essential to that flow. Encouraging questions, repeating student questions so everyone can hear, answering patiently or directing students to ask you outside of class, and revising instruction based on student questions all contribute to student-centered learning.

Lesson Planning in the Student-Centered Classroom: Wrap-Up

Sometimes the key to moving from teacher-centered instruction to student-centered learning lies in lesson planning. I often tell my oral communication classes an anecdote about the importance of planning. This may be attributed to Winston Churchill, but I heard it this way: Once, the pastor of a church was asked to give a speech to some members of the community. He agreed, but he said, "If you want me to speak for ten minutes, I need two weeks to prepare. If you want me to speak for twenty minutes, please tell me one week in advance. If you want me to speak for two hours, I'm ready now."

This always gets a laugh, and my students promise to spend a lot of time preparing their ten-minute speeches. But can't the same anecdote apply to lesson planning? If you want me to talk for an hour about the passive voice, drill some past participles, and assign some homework, I'm ready now. If you want a class that begins with an interesting warm-up; has a succinct explanation of passive voice; contains some controlled practice; something engaging and communicative, and some application with authentic materials—with comfortable pacing—then I'll need an hour or more to put this plan together!

As we have seen, lesson plan templates or textbooks that have a good progression of explanation/exercises/activities can be useful, but teachers know that they have to craft plans for their short-term and long-term goals, taking into consideration what their students can do and need to do, allowing time for questions, and indeed finding ways to encourage questions. Planning for flipped classrooms may be more challenging, as we have to resist the urge to reteach what (presumably) students have learned on their own.

Veteran teachers often save and re-use plans—but seldom in exactly the same way twice. I always say that teaching ESL never gets boring. In a student-centered classroom, I plan for how to teach my students, not how to teach the subject.

Making Connections

Challenging Beliefs: What Teachers Think

What's your opinion? Circle the extent to which you agree or disagree with this statement. To read survey responses to the statement, please turn to Appendix 1 (pages 178–179).

> I may be in control of the exercises and activities that students do in my class, but I am not in control of what they learn.
>
> strongly agree   agree   neither agree nor disagree   disagree   strongly disagree

Classroom Connections: What Teachers Do

In a class you are teaching or visiting, you may want to consider some of these points about how the lesson is planned and how the plan is carried out.

1. Is there a written plan for the class? If yes, how detailed is it?
2. Is the agenda written on the board? Are the goals for that day's class clear to the students?
3. Does the plan change during the class? (Note: If you are visiting the class, this may not be evident unless you interview the teacher.)
4. Is there any assessment taking place?
5. Does the flow of the class resemble the lesson plan format from Chapter 3?
6. Is the classroom flipped? If so, to what extent?
7. Are patterns or class routines evident? If so, do the students seem comfortable with them?

8. How are students who work at different paces accommodated?

9. Are there any activities or games?

10. How are students' questions handled and/or encouraged?

Strategies and Motivations: What Teachers Say

Consider these comments from survey respondents on a few of the topics from this unit.

On striking a balance between planning every moment of a class and being spontaneous:

Most teachers have a general idea of how they want any particular class session to unfold, and they know the value of writing out their ideas in a plan along with readying handouts, PowerPoints, video clips, and so on. But as teachers gain more experience, they are more open to letting learning experiences happen in the class.

Kay Marshall: "I usually teach a better class if I have a lesson plan, though I sometimes am a little too 'controlling' and later realize that the students would have benefitted more if I had deviated from my plan and followed a topic or activity that 'evolved' during the class that students were responding to (and learning from) particularly well. With more experience, I have learned to trust these instincts more and change course from time to time."

Stephanie Sareeram: "I always have an outline for each class—I wouldn't say I have a full-blown lesson plan. I find that when I plan each detail, the class is stilted and often flops. When I have a path of tasks to complete but wiggle room along it, class is more spontaneous and alive."

On using a lesson plan format (or requiring that teachers in your program use such a format):

A popular lesson-plan format includes five steps: Warm up or review, presentation of new material, controlled practice, free practice, and evaluation. While this progression may happen in some of our classes, if we force ourselves to fit our lessons into this format we may find this limiting and repetitive.

Mike J. Waguespack: "I think this kind of lesson plan is acceptable, but it can easily get in the way of more 'organic' instruction which rises out of students' level of understanding and preparation from previous class lessons. It also assumes that language instruction can be 'chunked' neatly, and that all language content can/should be presented in a similar way. I don't agree with this. There are some times when I want students to just see some language and 'dig' to find the rules/patterns on their own first."

Til Turner: "This organization is helpful in that it can prevent a lecture-heavy class. However, classes should be holistic and fluid, and if students want to spend a great deal of class time asking questions for clarification or practicing writing, it is useful to abandon plans and 'go with the flow.'"

Sherlie Scribner: "This plan assumes that each class is a discrete entity; however, in reality classes that meet daily have more 'flow.' Students who are practicing and testing themselves on grammar online outside of class at their own pace may come to class with questions about the work they have completed. I then decide whether they need additional practice to proceed."

Megan Calvert: "Variety is key! Meaning that if you do one thing too long, you'll lose your students. It doesn't mean you can't repeat the same types of activities or that you can't have predictable routines to streamline things. But a little bit of whole class work, a little bit of individual work, a little pair work, and a little group work—that's the kind of variety students need."

Nigel Caplan: "Every lesson is different; many are not self-contained, and it's more important to design activities and lessons that respond to the needs of the students and help them work towards the course learning outcomes. In fact, those outcomes/objectives should be on this formula if we're going to teach it to novice teachers."

On keeping goals in mind when planning lessons:

Many ESL teachers teach multiple courses in one semester, sometimes at more than one school. I usually teach four classes a semester, and each meets two times a week. I tell my friends who are not teachers, "I have eight inflexible deadlines per week." Given the pace of having to plan and execute so many classes in a short time, it can be easy to fall into a pattern of looking only at the short term, of cobbling together a handful of activities to keep students occupied. To guard against this, it is essential to keep the long-term goal or goals of the course in mind when planning every class lesson.

Lori Ward: "The most important principle to me is keeping the end goal in mind. How will the students be assessed? What is necessary to know, big picture, about what I've taught? I want to keep the content I teach streamlined with the end in mind, not bogged down in too much detail."

Dana Kappler: "I have short-term goals and long-term goals. A short-term goal might be for the students to learn about putting a period between two independent clauses and recognizing those clauses. A long-term goal is to have them begin to correct their punctuation in their writing."

Brian Anthon: "Every instructor needs to have the final goal in mind. What do students need to know and be able to do by the end of the course? Plan backwards from the end of the course for pacing and account for activities and information the students will need for a skill and knowledge base. Design assessments that will help them monitor their progress, and give feedback to all of them for improvement by the end of the semester."

On how our L2 experiences shape our teaching styles:

Many ESL teachers have studied (and still study) other languages, and of course for some English is their second language. These experiences give us a range of perspectives on what it means to be a second-language learner.

Nataliya Schetchikova: "English is my second language, and I've benefitted from what I've learned, but I teach differently from how I've been taught."

Elizabeth Rasmussen: "Whenever I feel impatient with a student's lack of progress, I open my Turkish textbook."

Nina Liakos: "I enjoy learning a language for its own sake, whereas the majority of my students view English as a tool that is necessary if they are to achieve their academic goals. We have different motivations, and what worked for me may not work for them. Still, I like to share strategies that worked for me, in case they might help."

Tom Hilanto: "Studying a foreign language and being expected to perform at a native level in reading, writing, listening, and speaking is a humbling experience. Every ESL teacher should have gone through that experience at least in one foreign language before they are allowed to teach ESL."

On students who dominate by asking a lot of questions:

We need to keep in mind that our students are often new to U.S. classroom culture, and this is reflected in how many questions they feel free to ask in class. They may be rewarded in other parts of their lives for asking a lot of questions, such as at work, while shopping, and so on.

Antonina Rodgers: "When one student is asking a lot of questions, he or she may not be aware of class dynamics and may not be willing to 'share the learning space.' It is a difficult habit to unlearn and could require a couple of counseling sessions so that a student learns that there could be different ways of obtaining answers to questions beyond asking all of them right there in the classroom."

Celia Leckey: "Even if one student asks all the questions, the others are probably glad she or he is. Some cultures actually designate a rep in a classroom situation—like Koreans. I had a class of all Koreans, and the oldest male did all of the talking. The second week of class an older male joined the group and took over as spokesperson."

On questions in a learner-centered classroom:

I once heard a teacher describe classroom management as a dance. Sometimes the students are in motion, sometimes the teacher. Balancing questions in the classroom is part of this dance.

Nigel Caplan: "Questions are good, but I don't want one student to dominate at the expense of others. All the other scenarios [in the survey] might be useful teachable moments. I believe in teaching the students, not the syllabus, so signs of not understanding or genuine curiosity should be encouraged. It's never inappropriate to ask a question I can't answer—that just means I need to find the answer."

Carol Ischinger: "There is usually at least one student who loves to talk and several who are happy to never participate. I need to make sure everyone participates."

Tom Hilanto: "In a student-centered classroom the students are often working in groups or pairs while the teacher walks around to facilitate the task at hand. The teacher should be able to field any questions of an individual or group without disturbing the flow of work for the other students. If the teacher feels the question is relevant to the entire class, she can then request the students' attention and address the question with the whole class. This is the great benefit of designing a collaborative class."

Unit Three:
Pair and Group Work in the Student-Centered Classroom

Asking students to work in pairs and small groups is at the heart of a student-centered approach to language teaching. When I first started teaching, I was trained in the audiolingual method. After a year of trying to get students to memorize dialogues and engage in drills (choral repetition! substitution drills! transformation drills!), I knew there had to be something else out there. I quickly discovered the communicative approach to language teaching and became an early adopter. People may speak of paradigm shifts in ESL teaching today. Is it communicative? Is it collaborative? Is it content-based? Is it task-based? Is it flipped? Are we accommodating learning styles or teaching to multiple intelligences? Compared to the shift from the audiolingual method to the communicative approach, these other "shifts" seem more like "tweaks" to me as they all effectively engage students in pair and group work that is collaborative, communicative, or both.

An overarching reason for putting students in pairs or small groups in our ESL classes is because the "subject" that we teach is not a subject at all. It might not be so necessary for a teacher of Biology, Geography, or History to ask students to work collaboratively. But as language develops, the more it is used to create and sustain relationships, the more it becomes essential to create those opportunities in the classroom.

This is not to say that students immediately know the benefits of working in pairs and groups in their classrooms. Indeed, when students expect teacher-centered instruction, they are often reluctant to work in pairs or groups with peers. Teachers understand students' reluctance about student-centered instruction as they work to integrate pair and group work into their classes. Peer teaching thrives in a collaborative environment, but it doesn't happen automatically.

This unit examines ways teachers create pairs and groups, how they use textbook exercises with pairs and groups, and how they extend beyond their textbook with pair and group activities to create collaborative and communicative opportunities.

Chapter 6
Pairing and Grouping Students

All of the teachers surveyed reported having students work in pairs and groups. Many teachers use pair and group work in every class session, with most using pairs and groups in at least every few class sessions (see Figure 9). This chapter deals with techniques for pairing and grouping students and considers the pros and cons of short-term and long-term groups.

Respondents who checked "other" to this question in the survey (see Figure 9) tended to comment that their use of pairs and groups can vary depending on the skill area of the class, with a few people noting that they use pairs and groups more in oral communication classes.

> "I use groups or pairs when it seems to be the optimal way to achieve the goal. Sometimes that is several times a day, and sometimes a few times a week."
>
> *Nina Liakos*

Forming Pairs and Groups

In my classes, pair and group work is both planned and ad hoc. In addition, you may not be able to guess the skill area of my class by looking in my door, as I use the strategy pretty consistently. Yes, oral communication classes lend themselves to pair and group work, but I use pairs and groups just as often in my classes that focus on reading and vocabulary as in the classes that focus on composition and grammar. And even if I don't plan extensive group or pair work, as soon as I see attention flagging or feel that I'm leaning toward too much of a teacher-centered classroom, I quickly restructure an activity so that it

Figure 9

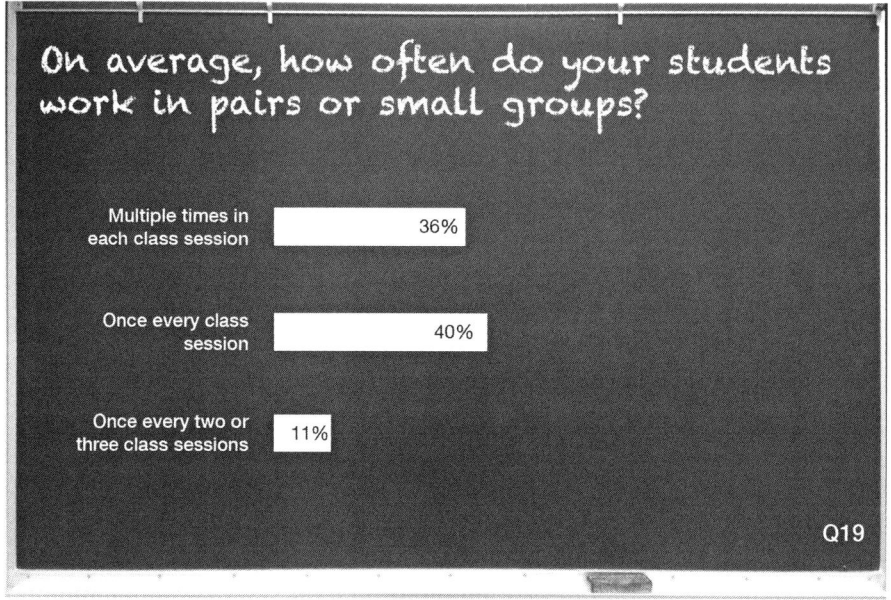

Note: Additional responses to this item appear in Appendix 3.

can be accomplished in a more student-centered fashion. Pair and group work is for me an antidote to both the too-quiet class and the too-noisy class!

When I cycle students into an ad-hoc pair activity, they normally just work with a neighbor. Indeed, 78 percent of teachers surveyed responded that they let students work with their neighbors (see Figure 10). In addition, some teachers let students choose their own groups even if they aren't sitting next to each other.

The benefits of this strategy are obvious. First, it saves time if students simply turn to each other or move their desks slightly. And if students are aware that they'll be asked to work with a neighbor, then they'll choose their neighbors wisely. This is especially important for shy students who may be reluctant to work with a stranger.

The pitfalls of allowing students to work with their neighbors are equally obvious. First, students who speak the same first language are often friends and often sit together. While they may promise to speak English while engaged in their task, I worry that students with the same L1 will be stuck in the same language patterns and won't be able to engage in as much peer teaching as I like. In fact, 70 percent of teachers

Figure 10

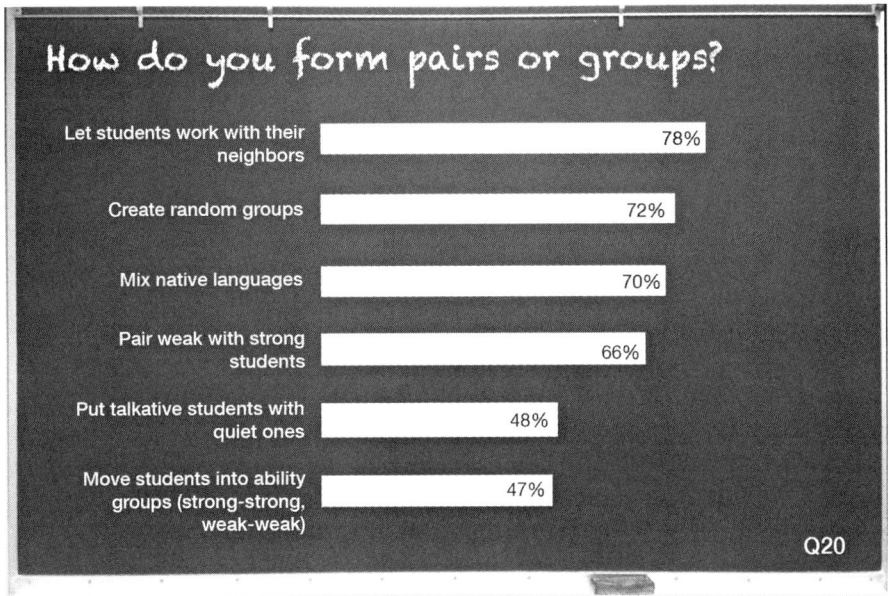

Note: Respondents checked more than one response; totals do not add up to 100 percent. Additional responses to this item appear in Appendix 3.

surveyed report mixing native languages when they pair or group students (see Figure 10). This can often be accomplished by simply having a student turn to face a neighbor on the right rather than the left, especially if your class understands that you want them to mix native languages.

However, even if L1 is not an issue, if we allow students to work with their neighbors each time we use pair and group work, friends may come to rely on each other too much—or more likely, a weaker friend relies too much on her stronger classmate. In addition, some students tire of working with people who sit near them, but they can't politely refuse. Their neighbors may work faster or slower or may be at a higher or lower proficiency level. When this happens, students look to the teacher to mix up the groupings a little. And finally, I worry about always allowing the back-of-the-room personality to work with another back-of-the-room dweller. My sense is the students who choose the back row are trying to hide from me. Indeed, I often find it hard to get all the way to the back of my crowded classroom to monitor the back row, so I like to cycle those people to the front on a regular basis.

> "One student in my listening/speaking class was reluctant to work with others. She was willing to share with the person next to her, however. I allowed her to stay where she was comfortable, and then after several sessions, I asked her if she was willing to work with another person, and she agreed. She enjoyed it, and she was willing to work with others afterwards."
>
> *Sherlie Scribner*

As previously mentioned, pairs and small groups are a great way to bring peer teaching into the classroom as well as even out pacing between fast and slow students. To that end, 66 percent of respondents report pairing stronger students with weaker students (see Figure 10). The pitfall of this strategy is pretty clear: Often the stronger students tire of being paired with weaker students. I have found that if the students aren't really aware of who I consider to be "stronger" or "weaker," then these pairings work well. With my population, often the very verbal student has more trouble with writing or with accuracy, so no one really knows who the stronger partner is. In other words, "stronger" and "weaker" and "faster" and "slower" can vary depending on the task. As Rebecca Wolff points out, some students might "have an over-inflated sense of their abilities." I find that pairing such students with the quiet, talented, worker-bee students is a nice reality check.

However, in cases in which the stronger student is much stronger than the partner, this practice can be problematic. In classes where I have one particularly weak student, I make sure that student works with a few of my strongest students on a regular basis. When I have more than a few weak students, this is more difficult to accomplish. In fact, by the end of one recent semester, my class had developed into two distinct groups. Half of the students were very dedicated—they worked very hard and made a lot of progress—while the other half really never reached their stride. In a desperate attempt to help the weaker students, I orchestrated strong/weak pairs in the last few weeks of the semester. I received lots of eye rolls and sighs from the stronger students, and the weaker students had fallen too far behind to be helped.

6 Pairing and Grouping Students 77

When creating strong/weak pairs, I believe that it's important not to let on that you are doing this. I use several strategies to create strong/weak pairs. In a composition class, if I have collected drafts in a previous class sessions, I can read the drafts before creating pairs for a peer review. I write the names of the pairs on the board and tell the students that I matched them based on the topic they chose or because there is something I want them to see in each other's writing. If students are getting into groups to discuss their journals in my reading class, I do the same. I usually construct groups of three and spread the weak students around. I tell the students that I matched them up based on the content of their responses to give each group some variety in their discussions (which is usually mostly true).

> "I take care to achieve diversity by gender, age, and country of origin."
>
> *George A. Flowers*

Sometimes I want students to complete a grammar, vocabulary, or reading comprehension exercise in groups of two to four. In order to create mixed-ability groups in a class of, say, 24 students, I make eight copies of the exercise and give them to the eight strongest or the eight weakest students. Then I say, "If you did not receive a copy of the exercise, please move to work with someone who did." This ensures that I have the strong or weak students equally distributed through the groups.

Sometimes I make my pairings look random when they are not random at all. I often ask students to find partners by giving them playing cards ("red 3, find black 3"), postcards that I've cut in half, a sentence that is cut in half—often into clauses—or a word plus definition. In each case, I give a pre-determined half to the stronger students. For example, strong students get the black playing cards, the left side of the postcards, the second half of the sentences, or the definitions. Weaker students get the other half. I move through the classroom quickly as I do this, so it really does look random. Students have to stand up, find their partner, and sit down together. It should be noted that this isn't a perfect system! It sometimes results in very "middling" pairs if I wind up with the weakest strong student paired with the strongest weak student.

Another point to keep in mind when pairing is personality type. In the survey, 48 percent of teachers surveyed noted that they strive to put talkative students with quiet students (see Figure 10). This can be a good strategy for encouraging shy students to work in groups. As DeAnna Coon points out, she generally tries to pair reluctant students with "the more outgoing students who can draw them out—the type you just can't ignore and who will get them talking in spite of their reluctance." These random-but-not-random strategies noted work just as well for this type of pairing: Talkative students can get the red playing cards and quiet students the black ones. How about mixing the back of the room with the front, or the window side with the door side? Similarly, one half gets the left side of the postcard, and the other half the right. In some of my classes, half of the class speaks the same native language. In that case, I'm usually up front about what I am doing. I say, "I'm giving the vocabulary word to the people who speak Amharic. Everyone else has a definition. Find your partner, check with me to see if you are right, write your word/definition on the board, and sit down together."

> "Mixing it up forces them to work with all levels of learners. I often use a weak/strong pairing, but random mixing also helps create a community. Sometimes though I do let them choose for themselves to give them a break and let them work with a classmate they feel comfortable with."
>
> *Kay Marshall*

Teachers don't always create mixed-ability groups: 47 percent of teachers reported creating groups or pairs of similar ability (see Figure 10). This was described in Chapter 2 as a strategy for dealing with students who work at different paces. Creating some strong groups and some weaker ones allows you to give more challenging tasks or extension exercises to the stronger groups while you sit down with the weaker students and help them along. I tend to use this strategy when I teach a lower-level class. I know my stronger students just need time on task with little supervision, and this gives me time to pay attention to the few who are struggling.

In addition to grouping by ability, Darlene Branges points out that we should consider pairing "students who stay on task and those who don't." While I generally strive to do this, in a recent semester I was pairing students for an oral presentation that required significant preparation both in class and out of class. I had two students who were somewhat less diligent than average in terms of doing homework and getting to class on time. I'd grouped them with more eager students earlier in the semester, hoping they'd learn by example. They didn't, so in this presentation they got to work with each other—and came to understand the frustration of working with someone who doesn't follow through.

Finally, 72 percent of teachers reported using random pairings and groupings (see Figure 10). I also do this often and am usually pleased with the way chance mixes up my students. Any of the techniques previously mentioned (playing cards, postcards, sentence halves, word plus definition) work great for creating pairs at random. If you want groups of three or four, bring sets of three or four playing cards or cut a set of postcards into three or four pieces. Teachers report other easy ways to create random groups. In the early weeks of the semester, they may ask continuing students to pair up with new students. Later on, you can simply ask students to find someone they've never worked with. Students can line up in some order—by birthdays, in alphabetical order by first name, by height—and then sit down in pairs. Students can count off (1 – 2 – 3), and then all of the 1s sit together, all of the 2s together, etc. Janice Hornyak reports that before the class begins she numbers the tables in the room 1 through 5. Then she stands at the door as students arrive and directs each to a table: first student to Table 1, and the second to Table 2. She notes that this is an easy way to separate friends who arrive together.

Short-Term or Long-Term Groups

Once pairs or groups are formed, how long do the students work together? Most teachers use short-term pairings (see Figure 11).

I generally only use longer-term groups when students are preparing group presentations or completing end-of-novel projects. However, I often ask groups formed in one class to continue working together in the next class. For example, if a group works on a written assignment together, I often collect, mark, and photocopy the papers for editing in the next class. They continue to sit together in the following class as they edit.

Figure 11

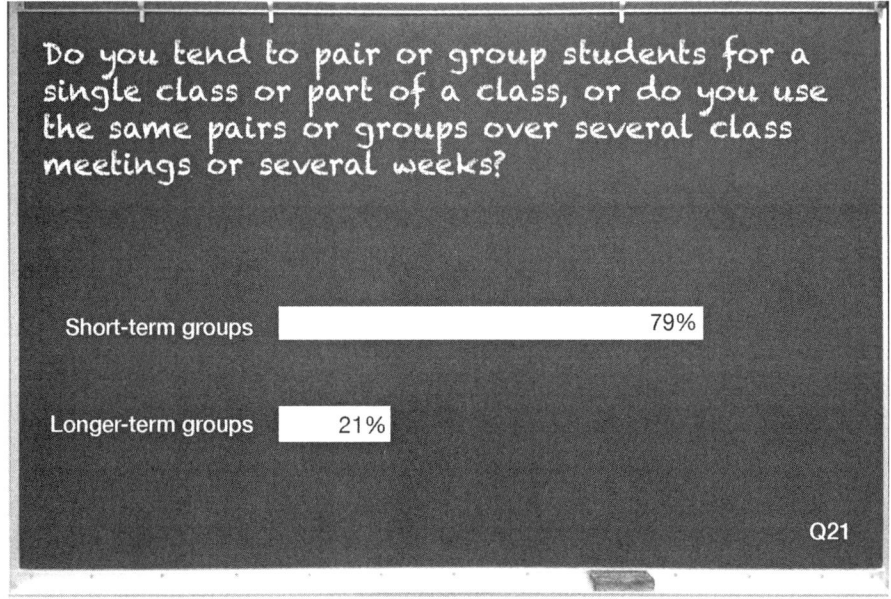

Janice Hornyak notes that she uses different configurations in different classes. While she often uses short-term groupings, she writes that in her advanced composition class, she likes to have "a 'working group' for each essay assignment, so groups work together for about three weeks (brainstorming, planning, peer-reviewing), and then switch up for the next topic."

In spite of this occasional use of longer-term groups, teachers tend to prefer short-term groups for several reasons. Nigel Caplan points out that his students "need experience talking to and working with many different classmates in order to be prepared for university life." And Vivian Leskes points out that "short-term groups allow students to bond with the entire class. No student gets stuck in a dysfunctional group for long." Indeed, Celia Leckey writes, "I don't want students to not want to come to class because they don't like their partner. For this reason, I change partners every day."

6 Pairing and Grouping Students

> "Sometimes I use long-term groups, too. For example, this semester students were reading books they had chosen themselves, and they met once a week to talk about how it was going. They met in the same groups all semester for the sake of continuity."
>
> *Nina Liakos*

Pair and group work is an integral part of student-centered learning, and teachers report very deliberate strategies for pairing and grouping students. We may ask students to move slightly to work with a neighbor or to move across the room to form a group, and we may keep students together for five minutes or five classes. Whatever we do, we must keep in mind the instructional benefit and the best use of class time and put ourselves in our students' places at times. It might be quickest to have a student simply turn to work with a neighbor, but is he the best partner for that student? It might be fun to have students participate in a complicated game-like activity to find partners, but is that the most effective use of class time? It might make sense to us to create long-term groups for both in-class and out-of-class work, but how do the students feel about this strategy? We must ask ourselves these and other questions as we set up pair and group work in our classes.

Chapter 7
Integrating Pair and Group Work with Textbook Exercises

Teachers report that students engage in more than a dozen kinds of activities while working in pairs and groups (see Figure 12). This chapter deals with how textbooks can be used in pairs and groups, including how to modify directions to be more collaborative and/or task-based.

Those of us who recall the paradigm shift from the audiolingual method to the communicative approach will recall that it was often up to the teacher to reimagine textbook exercises to make them more collaborative. Nowadays, many textbooks assume that students will be working collaboratively with at least some nod to pair and group work, either in

Figure 12

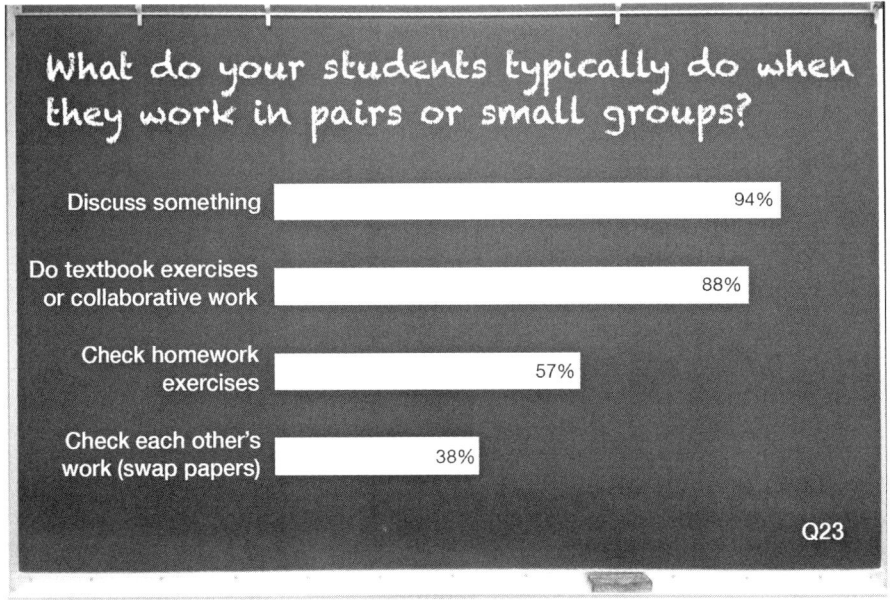

Note: Respondents checked more than one response; totals do not add up to 100 percent. Additional responses for this item appear in Appendix 3.

7 Integrating Pair and Group Work with Textbooks

instructions or within the construct of the exercises. This does not mean, however, that the textbooks do our work for us. Indeed, a quick review of the texts I often use shows that while instructions may suggest that students work in pairs or groups, spelling out exactly how that should be done would make instructions prohibitively long. Given the breadth of activities teachers report doing in pairs and groups, they are most certainly doing more than their textbook instructions dictate. In fact, it is clearly the teacher's responsibility to create opportunities for students to work cooperatively and collaboratively in productive ways with their textbooks.

Using Textbook Exercises for Class Discussion

In reading texts and texts that focus on listening skills, there is often a pre-reading or pre-listening exercise that asks students to discuss some questions with classmates, with a partner, and so on. Indeed, 94 percent of teachers surveyed reported using pairs or groups for conversation or discussion (see Figure 12). As previously mentioned, textbook instructions usually say something like "Before you read, discuss these three questions with a partner." To be honest, I never do this. The problem I see with this instruction is, then what? I much prefer an activity that includes a task to be completed. If I don't have a task or other very specific reason to have students work in groups, then I lead a whole-class discussion, often with the use of a PowerPoint. If I do indeed want to use pair or group work in a pre-reading or pre-listening exercise, I make the activity task-based. For example, I might create an anticipation guide, often based on the pre-reading questions in the text. Say my class is going to read an article on the high cost of weddings in the U.S. today. I might create an anticipation guide that looks like this:

AGREE	Big weddings are best. Couples should invite all of their friends and relatives to celebrate their marriage.	DISAGREE
AGREE	Couples should pay for their own wedding instead of asking their parents to pay for it.	DISAGREE
AGREE	Instead of paying for an expensive wedding, couples should save money for their future life together.	DISAGREE

I would then begin with a whole-class preview of the topic and article, hand out the anticipation guide, and allow for some quiet thinking time while students circle AGREE or DISAGREE. Since this anticipation guide is short, I can print it five to a sheet and cut it up so as not to waste paper. The completed chart can then be used as a bookmark, as students usually read for homework. This bringing in of a supplement, no matter how small, spices up the class a little and communicates to the students that we are not just working through the pages of the textbook. That is, it shows that I am teaching the students or the class, not teaching the textbook.

After handing out the slips of paper and giving students a few minutes to think, I would ask them to share their responses in groups of three or four. This would most likely be one of several group activities in this class session, so they should be sitting more or less with a group already. Their discussion would take no more than five to eight minutes and should center on whether they had the same or opposite opinions, or if they couldn't decide if they agree or disagree. There is no need to have an opinion yet; this is simply in anticipation of a reading to activate background knowledge.

As soon as the conversation starts to die down, I would pull the whole class back together for closure. I'd move through the three statements one by one and give each group a chance to report back briefly on any interesting comments that they had. This also should take no more than five minutes. At that point, they are ready to start reading the article or engage in other pre-reading exercises.

As mentioned, textbooks can't have such elaborate instructions even if they do use anticipation guides instead of open-ended discussion. It must be up to the teacher to construct this group experience for the class, and it's often up to the teacher to learn on her own how to do this. Claire Cirolia notes, "I decide on my own when and how students will work together. I think this is really an 'ESL thing' that I learned when I first started working in a literacy program and then in an adult education ESL program. It's completely ingrained in me now, but someone had to show/teach me this. It's never as simple as saying, 'Work with a partner.'"

Other instances of discussion questions in textbooks are often in the after-reading stage. Again, the instructions usually note that students

7 Integrating Pair and Group Work with Textbooks   85

should discuss the questions with a group. I generally use these exercises as written, adding some kind of follow-up to give the exercise closure. For example, if there are five discussion questions, I may break the class into five groups. I ask each group to discuss all five questions, but then toward the end of their discussion time, I give each group a number (1–5) and tell them to get ready to share their group's ideas on just that question with the class as a whole. They may appoint a reporter who will get ready to stand up and talk. Another way to add closure is to ask the students to choose one of the questions their group discussed for a short free writing or journal entry. Or you may ask the group to complete a graphic organizer based on their discussion. Completed graphic organizers can be shared with the whole class if you have a document camera, or you can tape them to the board or classroom walls.

In many programs in the United States and Canada, students don't lack for opportunities to engage in conversation with other non-native speakers of English. Perhaps our students are immigrants whose co-workers are other immigrants, or they are international students who live in a dorm or apartment with other international students. Or they just have lunch or break time with classmates. If there are enough language groups represented in your school, students have chances to converse with other learners of English in English. Keeping this in mind, I tend to avoid open-ended, unstructured conversation in my classes. If a school has a conversation partner program that brings native speakers into the classroom or student lounge, then, yes, unstructured conversation time is fine. Otherwise, I want conversation to be task-based or goal-oriented, to move the class forward.

One of the reasons I avoid open-ended conversation is because of an experience I still recall from my college Spanish class. Once a week or so we had an open conversation class—probably ten students or so. One assigned topic was to discuss a movie that we'd recently seen. I still remember my discomfort when I couldn't contribute to the conversation. Movie tickets were not in my budget, so I hadn't seen one since I'd arrived at college. This memory makes me bristle when I see topics in textbooks like "Discuss with a partner some things you like to do for entertainment on weekends" (What if my student works two 14-hour days on the weekends?); or "Talk about a time you or someone you know was in the hospital" (Well, what if that never happened to me or someone I know?). I understand some textbooks are eager to have students engage with the topics, but it's not hard to make discussions accessible to all and goal driven. Thus, many of my colleagues report that they routinely modify textbook directions on discussion topics.

Completing and Checking Textbook Exercises in Pairs and Groups

The survey showed that 88 percent of teachers have students do textbook exercises or other collaborative work in pairs and groups, and 57 percent report that they have students check homework exercises with a partner or group (see Figure 12). In these kinds of activities, again, textbooks may or may not mention working in pairs or groups in the instructions, leaving it up to the teacher to know how to orchestrate the experience.

> "Textbook authors don't have the information they would need to make appropriate recommendations for how I use the exercises in my class. They don't know my students or the make-up of the class, and they can't possibly understand the 'flow' or the pace I want to maintain in each class session, especially with integrated skills courses."
>
> *Judy Snyder*

Often textbooks may instruct students to complete an exercise with a partner. Instructions may say, "Work with a partner to make a list of X," or "Work with a partner to look up the meanings of these words which appeared in X." While these exercises are fine, the instructions do not tell what the students will then do with the list or the meanings of the words. If textbooks were to be more thorough, the instructions would not only be entirely too long but would take control of the flow of the class away from the teacher. It is, therefore, the teacher's obligation to come up with some closure for such exercises. If students work with a partner to make a list of X, then each pair might be responsible for writing two examples of X on the board for a whole-class wrap up or for

7 Integrating Pair and Group Work with Textbooks   87

the next step in a project. If partners are looking up meanings of words, they may be tasked with teaching those definitions to the rest of the class at the end of the activity.

In other cases, teachers ask students to work in pairs or groups on textbook exercises even when the instructions don't mention anything about collaboration. There are many ways this can be accomplished, but it's important to structure the activity so that students actually need to cooperate or collaborate. If students can just as easily do the exercise alone, why do it in a pair or a small group? We know the answer to this question, but often students don't, and you may see them sitting side by side, both working independently. As Dana Kappler points out, sometimes students feel that "they can do the job faster without a group and they don't want to have to put up with the dynamics of group work." Indeed, if students see a task as just an exercise to get through, they may not be eager to work together. If, instead, it is clear to them that negotiation and peer teaching are useful in language development, then students should be eager to work together, which is not to say that this isn't a hard sell at times, because it can be. Dorothy Gudgel notes that she "makes sure students understand what the learning task is that is expected of them" in order to structure a successful group-work experience.

> **"If the activity can be done** just as easily alone, I might have students in pairs take turns (one odds, one evens). While the one is answering, the other is the "coach." He/she has to give verbal feedback after each answer: 'I agree' or 'I'm not sure' or 'I don't think that's right.'"
>
> *Elisabeth Chan*

I generally strive to create situations that require collaboration. If students are writing sentences together, I often have one partner do the first half of the exercise, and then switch writers in the middle. I tell them that while Student A is writing, Student B has to talk, and in essence, dictate. Then the roles reverse. Both students put their name on the paper, so they have equal stake in the accuracy and share responsibility for proofreading at the end. If the exercise requires students to fill in blanks, I normally photocopy one per group or pair so the partners have to turn the paper in, rather than having them simply write in their textbooks. Again, they take turns writing and put both names on the paper. When I return the papers, I ask them to work together once again to review and correct any errors. As Virginia Cabasa-Hess points out, students soon see that "another pair of eyes is better than theirs alone." And Breana Bayraktar writes that if she finds students who are reluctant to collaborate, "I circulate, remind them that the task at hand is to do X with their group, and (if need be) stand over them until they start focusing on the task together."

> "Model pair work for students, so they will not end up doing it individually while sitting next to each other. Modeling also shows that the more important part of 'compare answers' is 'discuss why' or 'defend your answer.'"
>
> *Elisabeth Chan*

Students can complete exercises together, but more often we may have them complete them individually and check them together. A very common instruction in many grammar books and workbooks is "check your answers with a partner," especially in exercises where there is just one correct response. As with the instructions for discussions described earlier in the chapter, more thorough instructions would not only be too long but would restrict the teacher's freedom to structure the flow of the class as he sees fit. However, if one follows the "check your answers with a partner" instruction with no follow up, something will definitely be lacking in the lesson. What if both partners have the wrong response? What if two or three responses are acceptable? I generally like to add some mechanism for a check on accuracy to such situations. First, I tell students that if they agree, they are probably right. If they disagree on a response, they should discuss that item. Perhaps some peer teaching might take place. Finally, if they don't agree and can't come to agreement after discussion, they should mark that item and call me over. If several groups have the same item marked, that's a teachable moment, and I generally call the whole class together to discuss that item.

7 Integrating Pair and Group Work with Textbooks

After the pair checking is complete, my work is not done. I still allow for a final check on accuracy, and I have several strategies depending on the situation.

- ❏ If students have completed a short exercise, I may put a completed copy on the screen in the classroom and students check their own work. Similarly, pairs that finish fast might write responses on the board if they are short, such as with one-word responses. This is not to say I go through the entire exercise again, as that would be deadly. Instead, I ask students to do a quick visual check.

- ❏ If students have completed and peer-checked several pages of exercises, I may fill in one copy of the pages myself and tape them to the walls of the classroom. After they have compared and discussed, they stand up and move around as they check with my "key." Again, this happens very quietly after a noisy peer check time of reading exercises aloud.

- ❏ If students have completed several pages of exercises, after pairs or groups have had a chance to compare their work, I put each pair or group in charge of copying their correct responses onto a clean photocopy that I provide. If I have ten pairs, for example, I cut the photocopied exercises into ten parts. Once they are complete, we can share them on the document camera with a final group check on accuracy and practice proofreading. I'll say, "OK, here's page 21. Did the group get this 100% correct, or do you notice anything that needs to be fixed?"

- ❏ Finally, I often collect and check students' grammar exercises. Even after they've checked with a partner and engaged in some peer teaching, they still may have significant errors that they need to address. Having students review and check first reduces my grading time, however, since they often do polish up their work before I see it.

Even if students are just checking work they completed at home, they may be reluctant to work with a partner or in a group when linguistic accuracy is the focus of the exercise. As Nina Liakos points out, "Some students want teacher feedback all the time." I believe that since my students know that there will be a final check on accuracy by me, they are more willing to work on checking and peer teaching in pairs and groups.

> "I know that students who have done their homework do not want to work with students who haven't done their homework or students who haven't come prepared. They feel it's a waste of time. I have those unprepared students leave the classroom, though, and I don't let them participate."
>
> Lisa Stelle

Students also may be reluctant to work with a partner or in a group to check homework because they are not prepared for class. As Breana Bayraktar points out, "Sometimes students haven't done the homework, so they don't have anything to share or check. Sometimes they are really lost and (I think) don't want to share that they are lost." In these cases, I find using pairs or very small groups to be even more important. In my classes, yes, in the first few weeks some students think that homework is optional. However, if I put them in a small group to check their homework they not only see a model of how a more conscientious student works, but the (usually slight) embarrassment of not having anything to share motivates them to get it done the next time. In addition, my sense is that students are more likely to share that they are lost if they are working in a small group that I can chat with quietly during class. In short, a student-centered class does not allow for the amount of anonymity that some of our students seek! One cannot be a silent observer in a student-centered language class.

Some students may also be reluctant to work in groups on exercises or other collaborative work because they feel they are at a higher level in their knowledge of English than their classmates. Lauren Boone points out, "Some students feel they are better than others and don't want to be 'dragged down' by a partner of lesser ability." And Stephanie Harm notes that "some students feel that they have nothing to learn from their classmates either because they feel their skills are superior or because they feel that only the instructor can provide them with useful information." In cases like these, George Flowers explains, "Sometimes I attempt to sell a student on group work by appealing to him or her to take on a leadership role in the group because of his or her strengths in some area." Students come to see that explaining something to another student is a great way to learn.

> "Recently I had a very stubborn student who though he was better off alone for the first part of the semester. Then he learned that to do well in class, he had to participate in some group assignments. He also saw and was told that group work and effective social interaction is necessary for school and work life."
>
> *Christina Luckey*

Teachers who are committed to using pair and group work in their classes in order to make them more student-centered understand that collaborative work is not a way to supplement traditional resources like textbooks. Instead, they learn and share with each other strategies for how to reimagine exercises and rewrite instructions to make their textbooks function effectively for pair and group collaboration.

Chapter 8
Other Pair and Group Opportunities

While teachers work hard to tweak textbook exercises to make them more collaborative or tasked-based, they certainly do not limit the pair and group work in their classes to textbook exercises. In fact, it seems that many pair and group experiences in ESL classes have students engaged in tasks that are beyond the scope of their textbooks. This chapter describes some opportunities to move away from textbooks with pair and group activities.

Low-Risk Collaborative Activities

Low-risk activities help to introduce students to each other and to the concept of working in groups: 31 percent of respondents report having students read aloud to each other (see Figure 13). I do this quite frequently in my classes. I just make sure that the reading level of the passage is low—at the students' reading level or easier, and that the reading is something that is logical to read aloud—a story, say, rather than a magazine article.

While students are reading aloud, I move from group to group to listen in and help with pronunciation. I usually encourage students to switch readers at logical breaks in the reading, such as at the end of each paragraph. A low-risk activity such as this gives students who are new to group work a first experience with turn-taking. I encourage students to begin again and re-read in a different order until I come by and hear everyone at least once.

My students also read aloud while they are checking homework exercises. I never let them check true/false exercises by sitting in a group and saying: 1. True. 2. False. Instead, I insist that each group member take a turn to read an item aloud, followed by a statement like, "I think that one is true." Then I encourage the group mates to say either, "I agree," or "I disagree; I think that one is false." And then they discuss. I accomplish this by modeling. First, I model the wrong way (saying, for

Figure 13

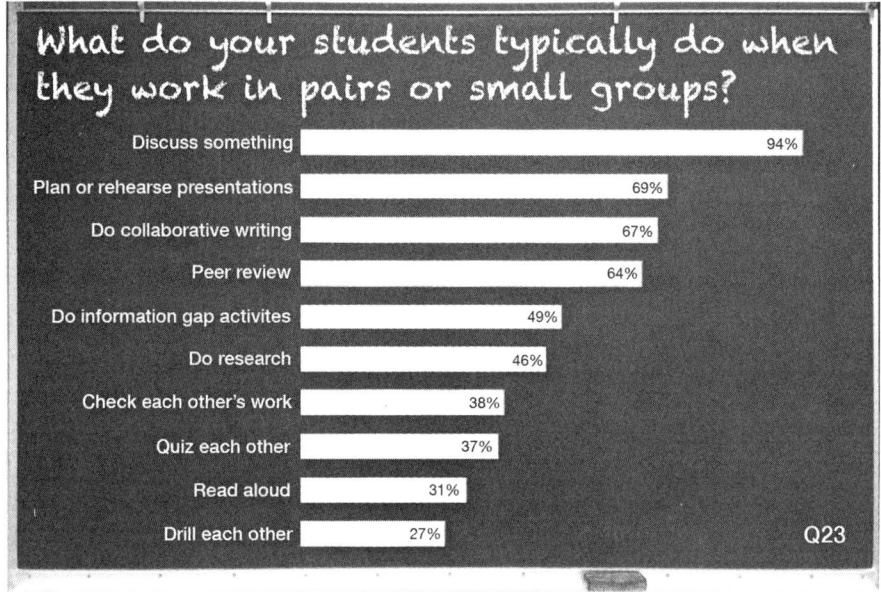

Note: Respondents checked more than one response; totals do not add up to 100 percent. Additional responses to this item appear in Appendix 3.

example, 1. c. 2. b.) and say something like, "Now that doesn't seem like I'm speaking English, does it?" Then I model the right way, either by role-playing alone or by recruiting a student to be my partner.

Once students are more comfortable working with each other, they can engage in activities like quizzing or drilling each other: 37 percent of respondents reported that their students quiz each other, and 27 percent reported that their students drill each other (see Figure 13). This technique works for some grammar points and for vocabulary, where acquisition depends on automaticity and memorization requires time on task. I frequently create, or ask my students to create, double-sided flash cards for grammar or vocabulary. While students may think they can quiz themselves or drill for memorization while sitting alone in the classroom or at home, I encourage pair or group work for its multi-sensory nature. Students say and hear what they are memorizing, often holding or sorting flashcards or small slips of paper, for example. They can also make a game or challenge out of the activity; having fun together creates important bonds.

Game-Like Communicative Activities

In many lower-level ESL classes, teachers structure pair activities to force communication in English in what have come to be called information gap activities. In this type of activity, Student A has some information that needs to be communicated to Student B, and vice versa. On the survey, 49 percent of respondents report using information gap activities in their classes (see Figure 13). When these activities are integrated carefully, they allow students to use English for communication with a focus on accuracy.

Information gap activities may be picture based, may use graphics, or may simply use words in a pair-dictation. Students can work in a back-and-forth fashion, or Student A can speak first while Student B takes notes or writes, and then roles switch. Information gap activities are great for practicing targeted vocabulary (clothing, food, places, numbers, and so on), survival skills (telling time, talking about money, and so on), and grammatical structures (*there is/are*, present or past verbs, imperatives for directions, and so on).

I believe that every ESL teacher should know how to construct and execute an information gap activity. It's important to me that such activities be integrated into my curriculum with a learning focus, so students don't see them as busy work or games. Working to integrate an information gap into a lesson illustrates to a teacher what skills and knowledge need to be pre-taught and shows her how to set up and model effectively—and what happens when she doesn't. While we can't control for all variables, we can do our best to prepare students for the task. If your beginning-level students are practicing telling time in an information gap, do you need to review pronunciation of numbers? If your students are using pictures from the produce section, have you taught names of fruits and vegetables? As George Flowers notes, "Most failures in pair work I have witnessed were attributable to inadequate preparation by the instructor."

The pitfalls of integrating information gap activities may not be evident until you try one. First, students have to sit so that they cannot see each other's papers, but so that they can hear each other easily. Instructions need to be complete but not overwhelming, and the task needs to be clear and challenging, but not too complex. The teacher has to move quickly through the room once the activity starts in order to see that everyone is on task and not simply showing each other answers or swapping their sheets, and to check that most of the communication is happening in English. In my classes, as soon as everyone confirms that they understand the activity, I fly through the room and always find at least one pair in which both students are looking at the page that is labeled Student A and can't figure out what they are supposed to do.

I also believe that every ESL teacher should engage in an information gap activity at least once, taking on the role of a student. There is a certain amount of tolerance for ambiguity that one needs to have to complete a task by listening alone. We need to know what this feels like to understand what our students are subjected to. If you are not sure if the task in your information gap is too complex, try it out with a fellow teacher. If you get confused, your students will too.

Information gap activities are sort of high stakes yet low stakes. They are high stakes in that communication must happen to complete the task, and they require a significant amount of investment by both Student A and Student B. They are low stakes in that they feel like games and no one is (usually) graded on the product. While testing might look similar to the information gap, students usually complete a test or quiz on their own after the information gap, so the activity itself can be seen as low-risk.

Group Work as Safe Haven

Once students are comfortable with each other, working in groups can be a safe place to take risks. It was previously described how students can check their homework with a group or partner before turning it in for the teacher to check. In addition, 38 percent of teachers responded that they sometimes have students swap papers to check each other's homework or a quiz (see Chart Q23 in Appendix 3). That way, students get instant feedback without having to rely on or wait for the teacher.

Another way to use a group as a safe place is to have students rehearse together. Any time students will need to stand up in front of the entire class and teacher—and possibly even a video camera—they can rehearse in a small group first. On the survey, 69 percent of respondents report that their students rehearse presentations, dialogues, role-plays, or reader's theater in groups (see Figure 13). Even if I ask one student to stand up and report on a group's conclusions, I usually encourage that student to rehearse with the group a few times. Claire Cirolia points out that allowing time to rehearse demonstrates that "we're all in the same boat and that the classroom is a safe place for all students to learn without being judged."

The group support doesn't have to end when the presentation begins either. At a recent conference, I heard this tip: During the rehearsal stage, have group members identify a couple of the speaker's behaviors. Is he swaying? Is he looking at only one part of the room? Is he speaking too softly, too quickly, or too slowly? Then two or three "trouble spots" are identified, and the group makes small signs to hold up during the presentation. The signs may say, "Eye contact" or "Slow down" or "Stand still." The group members then act as coaches and hold up a card when they think the presenter needs a reminder.

I've recently added some technology to group rehearsal time. My school has a set of iPads that I can bring to class, and students use the camera feature of the iPad to record each other as they rehearse their presentations. After the rehearsal, they watch and critique themselves, and then delete the recording before turning the iPad in. I've also noticed that they record themselves using their smart phones so that they can take the recording home to review. In addition, having these recording devices in their groups also allows them to record me as I visit their group. Recently students were practicing reading poems aloud in groups, and as I visited each, I offered to read their poems once while they recorded me with their phones.

Pairs and Groups in Writing Classes

One of the major uses of pairs and groups today is in our writing classes—across many levels. Indeed, pair work can be woven in to many steps in the writing process.

On the survey, 94 percent of respondents report having students discuss, interview each other, or brainstorm topics for writing in groups (see Figure 13). These activities are critical in the first steps of the writing process. I often use think-pair-share when brainstorming topics. In addition, in my intermediate writing courses, students interview each other for one composition and often interview me for another.

8 Other Pair and Group Opportunities

On the survey, 46 percent of respondents report having students do research in pairs or groups (see Figure 13). While this may take place in a reading or oral communication class, often research leads to writing. I have had students do a small research project in groups and present "quotable quotes" in PowerPoint presentations as a step before writing a documented essay.

Another 67 percent of respondents report having students write collaboratively (see Figure 13). Again, this might be in any skill area. For example, in a reading class students might create questions on a passage collaboratively, or in an oral communication class students might write a dialogue collaboratively. I use collaborative writing frequently in my writing classes. My students have produced everything from a complete, short piece in my lower-level classes to group-written body paragraphs as part of a whole-class essay exercise in my upper-level classes.

Students peer review each other's writing in 64 percent of respondents' classrooms (see Figure 13). I like to keep a few points in mind as I prepare peer review opportunities for my students, no matter what the level. First, I prefer to use peer input at the review/revise stage rather than at the editing stage. My students are not always good editors of their peers' writing. I also keep peer reviews very short and task-oriented. Students usually give three or four pieces of input, often in writing but also followed up with some conversation. I generally see the benefit in the *reading* of a peer's paper, so I usually just create the task to give some focus. I also often do peer review in a round-robin form, so each student gets to read papers written by several classmates. Sometimes my round-robin peer review uses final drafts, again because I think the value is more for the reader than for the writer. In one round-robin peer review, the task is to write a compliment to a classmate about his or her draft, and staple a note to the back of the paper (so others can't read it). This kind of peer review shows students that there are many ways to address a writing prompt successfully. This is often a good end-of-semester activity.

Pairs and groups can be a way for students to become comfortable using their second language to accomplish real tasks. If our students are new to our programs, this may be the first time they've engaged with English outside of a textbook, and so we give low-risk activities. They can be a way to make memorizing easier and fun as well as to create a safe haven for some risk-taking. And group brainstorming as well as peer review in pairs or groups are critical components of process writing.

Pair and Group Work in the Student-Centered Classroom: Wrap-Up

Two major reasons that are often cited for using pairs and groups are to increase students' time on task and to even out differences in pacing. In a teacher-centered environment, a class of 20 students checks a 20-item exercise by reading each item aloud, and each student is responsible for one item. In a pair, each student is responsible for ten items—increasing exposure to the language, and time on task, tenfold, and increasing the chance that some peer teaching will take place. In addition, as was previously noted in Chapter 2, teachers pair students in a variety of ways to help slower students work faster and to slow down students who work too fast (and perhaps carelessly).

In addition to increasing time on task and promoting peer teaching, teachers know that having students work together encourages them to be responsible for their own learning, fostering more independence than we see in traditional teacher-centered classrooms. Furthermore, allowing students to work in pairs or small groups may encourage them to take more risks. A student who is reluctant to speak up in front of a large group for fear of making a mistake is more likely to take that risk with a peer, especially one who is part of a supportive learning community.

No one has to convince ESL teachers today to use pairs and groups in their classes. However, no two teachers use pair and group work in exactly the same way. Teachers develop their preferences with their student population in mind, find their comfort zone, and bring their own styles to integrating pair and group work into their classes.

Making Connections

Challenging Beliefs: What Teachers Think

What's your opinion? Circle the extent to which you agree or disagree with this statement. To read survey responses to the statement, please turn to Appendix 1 (pages 180–181).

> Sometimes students just go through the motions and are not really engaged in learning.
>
> strongly agree   agree   neither agree nor disagree   disagree   strongly disagree

Classroom Connections: What Teachers Do

In a class you are teaching or visiting, you may want to consider some of these points about pair and group work.

1. Do students work in pairs or groups? If so, for what portion of the class?
2. How are pairs or groups formed? What considerations are taken into account when pairing or grouping students? (Note: If you are visiting the class, this may not be evident unless you interview the teacher.)
3. Are pairs or groups short-term (for this class session only), or do they continue from a previous class session or to a future class session?
4. Do students work with their textbook(s) in pairs or groups?
5. Is the pair or group work modeled? If so, how?
6. Does the pair or group work require collaboration? If so, how?
7. Do students work with supplemental (not textbook-based) materials in pairs or groups?
8. Do students engage in peer review of writing or collaborative writing in their pairs or groups?

Strategies and Motivations: What Teachers Say

Consider these comments from survey respondents on a few of the topics from this unit.

On avoiding using long-term groups:

Many teachers know that for long-term projects like group presentations and other work that needs out-of-class group work, they have to create some long-term groups. However, for several reasons they find long-term groups to be problematic.

> Stephanie Sareeram: "I am wary of using long-term groups because of my own terrible experiences with them when I was a student. I like the students to feel that they aren't stuck. Having the freedom to work with new people takes a lot of strain off. I'm probably projecting a lot, but that's why my preference is for short-term groups."
>
> Mike J. Waguespack: "I don't care for long-term groupings because students tend to find their preferred role (leader/follower, busy bee/slacker) and get too comfortable. By changing the groupings more often, I hope they are questioning their position in the group so that they 'try on' a number of roles and responsibilities."
>
> Judy Snyder: "I really want my students to create a community, and being in a long-term group can cause some students to become very dependent on each other. Also, if a group member or two is absent, this upsets the balance."

On students' reluctance to work in groups and on helping students overcome their reluctance:

Teachers are aware that many students come from educational systems that value a teacher-fronted class, and that this may cause some reluctance to work collaboratively. In addition, age, gender, and personality issues also come into play when students are asked to work with others whom they would not generally have contact with outside of class.

> Therese Kravetz: "Some students are shy and some are afraid of making a mistake. Others don't understand the point of working in a group, so that has to be clarified."

Til Turner: "I tell them that we are in a friendly environment in which everyone can help everyone else progress and that each student has something original to offer."

Tom Hilanto: "The reluctance comes, I believe, when there are not clear outcomes or a purpose for the group work. But collaboration will be a key skill that will transfer to the workplace, and many of their future co-workers will have points of view and personalities that will conflict with their own. To succeed, they will need to learn how to work well with a variety of opinions and personality traits."

Lori Ward: "They often see themselves as perfectly able to do activities by themselves and see working with others as a burden. I tell them that I understand how they feel as I used to feel the same way, but I have come to learn that working in pairs or groups helps my learning in unexpected ways."

W. Riley Holzberlein: "I require them to find a partner to work with because I feel working with others is both an important academic and professional skill which requires some practice."

Robyn Brinks Lockwood: "It's a hard truth, but their future professions and life in general are full of situations in which we have to talk or work together. I let my students know that it's better to practice here in the safety of the classroom."

Lisa Stelle: "For the shy students and the ones who are worried about their pronunciation, I tell them that we all have accents and that everyone struggles to make the correct sounds. I explain that that is why they are in school—to learn and improve on the things that cause them trouble. I also make sure they know that no one will laugh at them or make fun of them when they speak. That is absolutely not allowed in my classroom. Everyone knows they are there to support each other."

Mike J. Waguespack: "A few students have told me that they see no reason to work with classmates since their classmates' English is no better than their own. However, the most common comment I get from students about pair and group work is that they feel it is one of the most valuable elements of my classes, since they get to share ideas and perspectives and help each other to understand."

Unit Four: Classroom Interactions

A random look inside a student-centered ESL class might reveal any number of scenarios, from something as traditional as a teacher speaking and students taking notes to students working quietly in groups, to everyone out of their seats moving, talking, and writing all at once. In all but the first scenario, an untrained observer may wonder what is going on in the class and if the teacher is in charge or has lost control. My answer to that observer would be to come into the class and stay a while. She will soon see that the teacher is managing all of those interactions.

Even a trained observer might wonder about a teacher's choices if she just peers in without understanding the dynamics of the group and the goals of the class. Indeed, there is a place for everything in a student-centered class. Sometimes a class might seem quite teacher-centered, with a teacher lecturing, showing, and modeling. Sometimes a class may seem to be flying on auto-pilot as students work in groups and the teacher hangs back to avoid interfering in their negotiations. Other scenarios may have teachers walking among groups of students or sitting with them in a circle. In any of these cases, teachers have made conscious decisions about what is happening, when it happens, how long it lasts, and more. This unit examines the choices teachers make about class interactions.

Chapter 9
Teacher Places, Teacher Talk

Direct, teacher-centered instruction must be part of student-centered learning. While the new approach of "flipping" moves some or all of the direct instruction out of the classroom, many of us still present or review material in a teacher-fronted format. Indeed, students expect and deserve well-planned presentations of new material or succinct reviews of instruction, whether from a previous class or on their own in a flipped class. This chapter deals with the many decisions teachers make, either conscious or unconscious, about how they present or review material in such situations.

Your Place in the Room

At a conference several years ago I heard a teacher giving some advice on where and how a teacher should stand in the classroom. Her opinion was that teachers should stand as still as possible when presenting information so that students would not be focused on watching the teacher move around the room instead of on the subject matter. I had never thought about that before and was eager to hear what other teachers had to say on this point. I found that teachers have well-supported opinions about their spot in the room—even though there is clearly not one answer to this question.

Many teachers like to stand in one place when they present information. Of course no one teaches exactly the same way from one day to the next, but many teachers report that at least sometimes they stand at a board or screen (81 percent), or behind a computer or other device like a document camera (60 percent), when they teach (see Figure 14). You will find me in one of these two places when I'm presenting something new to my students. I like to let the visual—my graphics, diagrams, examples, and so on—be at the heart of my explanation. Ruth Takushi

Figure 14

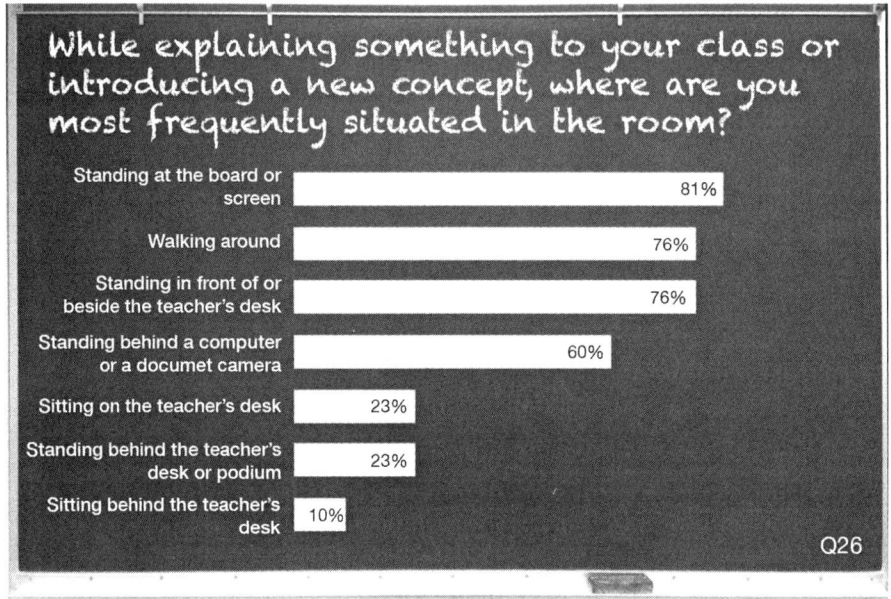

Note: Respondents checked more than one response; totals do not add up to 100 percent.

explains, "I try not to walk around too much when introducing a new concept. I think it's distracting." I may even sit down for a bit if I am writing or drawing on a document that is on the document camera, to give everyone in the room a clear line of vision to the information on the screen. This, however, is not popular with teachers—only 10 percent reported sitting while explaining something (see Figure 14).

Teachers who stand at the front of the room while explaining have clearly thought through this issue and have made a deliberate choice. Cheri Bridgeforth notes, "I feel that being at the front while introducing a concept helps students focus their attention." Megan Calvert adds, "Your body language alerts students about when they need to give you their attention." Also, as Christina Luckey points out, "I often have visual cues that I'm referring to." DeAnna Coon notes that she prefers to stand at the front of the room because "it's easy for me to see the students' faces and reactions and if they are paying attention, as well as easy for them to see me and what I'm signaling on the board or document camera. I generally gesture a lot, draw arrows on the board, point at the document, so I obviously can't do this if I'm walking around or sitting behind a desk."

This is not to say that standing still at the front of the room is the only way to present information. Even though he generally stays near the front of the room, Mike J. Waguespack says, "I tend to be a demonstrative instructor, so I move around a lot. Even if I am working from the computer or document camera, I will normally be darting back and forth to the board, students' desks, etc."

> "**Delivery is very important,** so I like to be front and center to maintain the students' attention."
>
> *Dawn Titafi*

Some teachers are less tied to the front of the classroom and to visuals while explaining a new concept than I am. Many of us teach in traditional classrooms that have a teacher's desk or a podium in the front of the room, but only 23 percent of teachers report standing behind the desk or podium (see Figure 14). In fact, the desk or podium is often seen as an unwanted barrier between the students and the teacher; 76 percent of teachers responded that they often stand in front of or beside the teacher's desk while explaining something or introducing a concept, and an equal number responded that they usually walk around the room during that part of their lessons (see Figure 14). George Flowers writes that he moves around "to be more engaged with the students," and Michele Rivera thinks "it generates energy to walk around the classroom." Also, Leslie Sheen writes, "I like to walk around if I can because it seems more relaxed and friendly."

Antonina Rodgers urges teachers to be active while giving explanations. She writes, "I believe that an active teacher will better keep students' attention. I also believe that each class session is a mini 'performance' through which students will understand and remember what they are learning. Students are also less likely to hide behind other students or engage in activities unrelated to class."

> "**Even though I am the 'expert'** in this scenario, I still believe that teaching is give and take. Sitting or standing behind a desk creates a barrier (physical as well as psychological) between the teacher and the students."
>
> *Judy Snyder*

Blackboard/Whiteboard Use in Direct Instruction

While many teachers have access to a variety of resources, from PowerPoints to YouTube to document cameras, many of us still use the blackboard or whiteboard to present material. Stephanie Sareeram points out, "If I'm teaching something new, I like to write on the board. I like board writing because I can use students' ideas. It's more spontaneous that way, and the explanation is more tied to them as an individual class." Similarly, I like my explanations to be organic—to start simple and grow to fill the board. I am sensitive to my students who are visual learners, so I like to craft the visual support carefully. Therefore I like to keep a few points in mind regarding the use of blackboards / whiteboards.

First, I like for there to be set places on a board for certain information. I write the day's agenda in the same place every day—a place that I might not have to erase right away that won't get covered up if I pull the screen down. Similarly, any notes about homework or upcoming tests, etc., tend to be written in the same place each time. If I have a spot by the door, that's where I write these check-on-the-way-out notes.

If I have a room with a whiteboard, I make sure that I have a variety of colored markers. Then I use the colors in some systematic way during my explanation. If I have to use chalk, I just have to be more creative with circles, underlines, and arrows.

Finally, don't forget to erase the board frequently between the parts of your class. Of course, I don't erase without giving some warning. I sometimes ask, two or three times, "Is it OK if I erase this?" while holding the eraser in the air. But then I do erase everything that is not necessary for the next part of the lesson. There is nothing more confusing to me than seeing information from some warm-up or previous part of the lesson—or worse, from a previous class—still on the board after the class has moved on to a new topic, or to see a teacher continue to add notes, definitions, instructions, and so on to an already-full board.

I usually expect students to take careful notes during or after my explanations. Sometimes I even bring blank, unlined paper for them if I want them to copy a graphic. However, recently I've started photographing my blackboard or whiteboard with my smart phone or tablet, especially when I've drawn a lot of graphics or used a lot of colors on something that students might want to study. I can then post the photo online for them to review at home. If students know I'll post our notes, then they can participate in the lesson without having to copy everything that I write on the board. Sometimes it's a give and take between training students to take notes and training them to rely on new technology.

Teacher Questions in Direct Instruction

In a student-centered classroom, teachers often view explanations as more of a give and take than a one-way delivery of information. As Breana Bayraktar points out, when she is explaining something new, "I am either writing on the board (but avoiding writing too much, for too long) or walking around doing Q&A to get the student to come up with answers themselves. I try my best to avoid lecture and instead ask questions."

Using questions to guide an explanation is often very effective in a student-centered environment. Something to avoid, however, is asking a lot of questions that you know the answer to. This sets up the teacher as the knower of knowledge, in my opinion, and makes the class feel like a guessing game. While some may see this as a distinction without a difference, I try to limit myself to genuine questions in the classroom and try to stay away from questions that I know the answer to.

Consider this (fictitious but possible) exchange:

Teacher: When do we use the past progressive tense?

(Teacher wants students to say that *we use past progressive tense to talk about a longer action in the past that was interrupted by a shorter action.*)

Student A: When we have *was* and then the verb has *–ing* at the end.

Teacher: No. Anyone else?

Student B: When we talk about the past.

Teacher: No. Anyone else?

Student C: When the action was continuing.

Teacher: No.

In this painful exchange, the teacher answers no because she is waiting for a particular explanation—perhaps one that students studied or were supposed to have learned. However, Students A, B, and C, weren't really wrong about past progressive; they were just not guessing where the teacher was going. If you ask questions like this, the answer may seem perfectly clear to you, the asker, but it can be quite frustrating for students. I generally urge teachers to visit other classes to view this guessing game from the students' perspective.

> Rebecca Wolff describes how she involves her students in her instruction: "I like to move around and ask questions while I'm explaining a new concept to keep students engaged and to gauge what they already know about a topic."

There is a simple fix to this. If you like to elicit information from students to guide your explanation of new material, instead of asking questions you know the answer to, ask questions you **don't** know the answer to. Since I became sensitive to this, it has been pretty easy for me to break myself of the habit—or at least lessen the frequency. I do not want to make my class seem like a game of "guess what teacher is thinking."

Therefore, instead of asking "When do we use the past progressive tense?" I ask, "Can anyone give us one reason we use the past progressive tense?" I honestly don't know if my class has studied that grammar point, so I really **don't know** the answer to the question. When I am using questions to guide instruction, I generally try to keep to this kind of question format.

Consider these examples:

❑ Don't ask: Why does *sitting* have a double *t* in the middle?
   Instead, ask: Who remembers why *sitting* has a double *t* in the middle?

❑ Don't ask: What does *crucial* mean?
   Instead, ask: Does anyone know what *crucial* means?

❏ Don't ask: Where does the comma go in this sentence?
   Instead, ask: This sentence needs a comma. Who can tell
                 me where it goes?

Again, perhaps a distinction without a difference, but I feel that these are more genuine questions that do not hold the teacher as knower of knowledge.

Of course, it is possible to ask the other kind of question in class (the kind to which the teacher obviously knows the correct answer), but perhaps in a review stage rather than when introducing new material. In that situation, I might preface my questions by telling the students, "OK, now I'm going to **quiz you** to see how well you know this." Thus, in a vocabulary class, I might say, "Each time I hold up a word, I want you to tell me what the suffix is and what part of speech the word is." Again, they know that I know, but since it's in a review situation and not during initial explanation, it seems more natural. Questions are a great way to include students in the process of learning, as long as they are a true give-and-take.

Modeling, Think-Alouds, and Scaffolding

Often when I am standing in front of my class, I'm not explaining something but rather engaging in modeling. I like to remind myself that it's human nature to want to follow a model or see an example. I try to remember to follow the pattern: "I do it. You do it together. You do it alone." That means I model the task, I have students try it in pairs or groups with my assistance, and then I ask students to try it alone.

As often as possible, I like to bring in student samples from a previous semester and very deliberately point out what is good about them. These could be essays, summaries, oral presentations that I've recorded, projects, and so on. Always get your students' permission to share their work; a simple piece of paper that explains how the piece will be used that the student signs and you keep should be enough, but you can check to see what your program prefers. And I always type up the work if it was hand-written, and clean up any surface errors without losing the student's "voice."

If I don't have student samples, I often create my own—especially for assignments like oral presentations. One benefit of creating my own sample is that I gain an appreciation for how challenging some of my assignments are. It may be easy to assign students to write a narrative of an important event that changed their lives in some way, but try writing that in 300 words!

In addition to modeling, it's important to scaffold instruction. As Ruth Takushi points out, "I always have to remind myself of the enabling skills needed to accomplish a larger task. Sometimes I forget a step and the students get confused or off track. Scaffolding is important, and I try to figure out what I need to explain and what the students can figure out for themselves." Take, for example, summary writing. Many of our EAP students summarize articles. It's important to see the enabling skills for that exercise and to lead students through finding main ideas, marking text, identifying transitions and examples, and so on. Such scaffolding is usually accomplished in a teacher-centered manner and can be flipped using PowerPoint or video.

I often combine scaffolding and modeling with think-alouds. For example, perhaps I want to model how to plan a composition from a class brainstorm that has resulted in a map of ideas on the board. In my think-aloud, I may say,

> "OK, I know that I want to have three body paragraphs, and I see that we brainstormed ideas in five general areas. I need to choose just three of those areas, or see if I can combine some of them. Hmm. OK, I think I'll use this one, and this one, and then combine these two into one paragraph [said as I circle groups of words]. Next, I need to decide which order to use. I think I'll work from general to specific, so, let me see. How's that? [and I write 1, 2, 3 above my circles]. Now I am ready to write my outline."

I also use think-alouds to model how I highlight text. I choose a short article—often I abridge an article, being sure to leave in what I want to call students' attention to. Then, I put the article on the document camera and read it aloud, stopping after each paragraph to "think aloud" about what I'm going to highlight or write in the margin. For example, I might say after reading the first paragraph,

> "Now I have read this entire article once, so I'm pretty sure this sentence captures the main idea. I'm going to highlight that and in the margin I'm writing 'main idea.'"

If I flip my classroom, these think-alouds can be recorded and posted for students. If I don't want to be filmed, I can point my camera at a sheet of paper and just film my hands writing or highlighting.

Explaining, questioning, modeling, and using think-alouds adds up to quite a bit of teacher talk. When I learned to teach with the audio-lingual method, teacher talk was central as we were to model every utterance and repeat correct utterances after our students. With the shift to the communicative approach, teacher talk became a bad word—a description of a poorly executed class is usually summed up with the phrase, "too much teacher talk." This is not to say, however, that a class with a silent teacher is our goal. Instead, teachers plan what and how much they will say in class, monitor themselves to deliver the direct instruction needed, and then move the focus back to the learners.

Chapter 10
Managing Student Interactions

As has been mentioned several times, group work is at the core of a student-centered classroom. The teacher-led or teacher-directed experiences in Chapter 9, for example, would most likely be preceded by and/or followed by pair or group work. Similarly, getting students out of their seats is another hallmark of student-centered classrooms. In all of these situations, teachers make carefully thought-out decisions about how these interactions happen. This chapter examines how teachers manage group work as well as whole-class interactions.

Managing Group Work

As teachers design and carry out activities, they make many decisions about their place in the room while their students are working together, and about their involvement in the pairs and groups (see Figure 15).

Most teachers like to move from group to group while their students are working, and they report having specific reasons for doing so. One good reason for doing this is to communicate to students that their group time is not wasted time and that their group work is not busy work. As Dan Branch explains, "I walk around to make sure that each group understands the lesson and is implementing it. I do not want them to ever get the impression that these activities are arranged so I can just relax or catch up on other work." One reason I don't like to have unsupervised and unstructured group work is because many of my students don't lack for opportunities to interact with other English learners outside of class. Group work needs a task and a purpose, and when teachers participate in the group work, students have confidence that they are working purposefully. As Brian Anthon notes, "An instructor should watch for groups that have difficulty getting started or those who are unclear as to what the task involves." Then you can step in and get everyone on the right track right away.

Figure 15

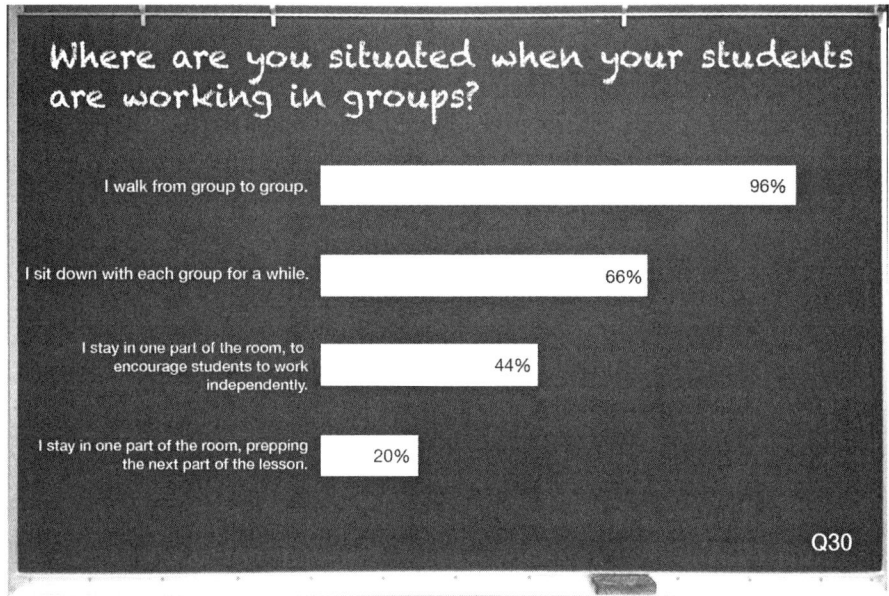

Note: Respondents checked more than one response; totals do not add up to 100 percent. Additional responses appear in Appendix 3.

Some teachers report that students, especially younger ones, don't always see how group work is connected to their learning goals. I make this clear by using exactly what students have worked on in groups when I construct their tests. For example, in my grammar class I have students practice past tense verbs by engaging in a pair dictation information gap that uses short anecdotes adapted from "stupid criminals" stories found on the Internet. Then, on the test they are presented with one of those anecdotes that I have rewritten in present tense which they have to change back to past. The task is not exactly the same as what they worked on in their group, but the content is the same—so the ones who were invested in the group work tend to do better on the test.

In another unit on using gerunds for activities, in a group exercise students construct advice for a variety of scenarios (*I don't have to work on Friday night. You should go dancing!*). Then, I present a few of the same scenarios on the test. In my composition class, if the students are to analyze a sample composition on a test, they will have done exactly the same analysis several times in groups before the test. This pattern, which they usually catch on to by the middle of the term, makes students take group work seriously.

> Jim Toepper describes the flow of group work in his classes. Sometimes teachable moments arise and he's able to pull the class together briefly: "I will give each group some time on their own to get started and comfortable with each other. I then will go from group to group to monitor progress and answer questions. If there is a common question or difficult instruction, I will address it from where I am in the classroom."

Putting students in groups is a great way to individualize instruction, and one way to make this happen is by circulating around the room while students are working together. As Brian Anthon continues, "Walking around is essential if you want to check on individual progress. A student who won't ask you a question from across the room will ask you when you're side by side." In my classes, I find that a student who is reluctant to speak very loudly will talk to me if I create a little "proximity bubble" with him.

As with every decision a teacher makes about the class dynamic, as Zaimah Khan points out, "it really depends on the purpose of the activity." Indeed, a casual observer may peer through the window of a classroom on any given day and find the teacher walking from group to group (as 96 percent of respondents reported doing at one time or another), sitting with a group (as 66 percent of respondents reported doing at least some of the time), or holding back to allow students to work independently (as 44 percent of respondents reported also doing at times) (see Figure 15). Often there is a combination. Lauren Boone notes, "I like to give them a few minutes to get going so they aren't intimidated, and then circulate and sit with each group for a while." Jane Stanga writes about another strategy: "I may just walk around and not approach any group. They are aware of my presence but I think sometimes they feel free to express themselves if I'm not standing right there. You can still see and hear a lot." Elaine George expresses this concept in a little different way: "I want my students to know I'm aware of what they're doing and that I'm available for help, but I don't like to 'hover' and make them feel embarrassed about expressing their ideas."

Teachers have equally compelling reasons for hanging back and not 'hovering,' as Elaine George points out. Robyn Brinks Lockwood notes, "This past term, in one class period I had groups preparing presentations. After sitting with each group for a time, I made an announcement that I was going to be at my desk in the front of the room if someone needed me. Members of the groups all called or came to my desk, so I think this might be a strategy worth exploring more." And Nigel Caplan notes, "Sometimes I deliberately keep away from them during group discussions and observe from the teacher's desk so that they don't become dependent on me."

In my classes, I like to hang back once I have circulated among the groups and know everyone is on task. I have several reasons for this. First, it is important for me that my students learn **how to learn** in my classes, so that their learning can continue outside of the class. If they believe that they can only learn when I participate, then their learning is limited to the classroom. I also want them to know what time on task feels like. I want them to experience what it feels like to engage in a task for an extended period, in English and without a teacher, so they are more likely to study and review outside of the class.

> Lisa Stelle describes her thinking about her place in the room while her students are working in groups: "During the first part of group work, I try to stay at my desk and busy myself with class prep. I want the students to work together to solve the problem or discuss the topic; I don't want them coming to me right away for help or with questions. They need to learn how to depend on each other and accomplish a task without me holding their hand. After some time has passed, then I begin going from group to group and checking in with them."

Sometimes I hang back at the beginning of the group work instead to let the students figure out roles and responsibilities without my interference. Then I circulate to check that everyone is OK, after which I may return to the front of the room.

Teachers seem quite unanimous when they describe their intentions for remaining at the front of the room while students work in groups. They report that this is a deliberate action to foster independence. Marilyn Odaka notes that if she stays in one part of the room, usually near the front, "I can discreetly make general observations of each group. Sometimes when a teacher is right next to a group, the group tends to become more self-conscious and/or inhibited." This may be more the case for shy students. It's good to give shy students space to contribute without fear of being judged or evaluated.

As a teacher who prefers a brisk pace to my classes, I often use group work time to set up the next activity. I might need to transition on the computer from something we were looking at on the Internet to a DVD, or get out my scissors and cut something up for sorting or reordering, or post something online that we did earlier in the class so that the students will have it for their homework. Sometimes I collect something in the first part of the class, such as an outline for a summary or a thesis statement for an essay. If I can use some class time to check these quickly and return them before the end of class, it seems like leaving students to work independently in groups for perhaps ten minutes is a good strategy. My students always know I can be interrupted even if I'm prepping or checking something. Janice Hornyak captures the flow of this when she writes, "If I am setting up the next part of the lesson, I'll walk around first and make sure they're all on task, then stop and prep, then circulate again so I know where everyone is in the assignment, and then go back and finish setting up." Group work time means there is little down time in the class while we transition to the next activity and get ready to continue the learning in homework time.

Finally, once we get student groups humming, how do we get the class back together? In my group work time, my students are usually very focused, and the room is quite noisy, so bringing group time to an end is sometimes a challenge. I usually try to give a warning ("OK, everyone, you have three more minutes. Three minutes!") and may set a timer on my phone or on the Internet, which I project on the screen. Then I give a second warning ("Please finish the sentence you are working on.")—and, of course, they don't stop. What then? Turning the lights off and back on sometimes gets their attention. You can also institute a routine in which students who are ready to transition quiet down and raise their hands. The group that is still working while the rest of the room is quiet, hands in the air, will transition pretty quickly. It's important for me to bring the class back together for some closure after group time, and I'm always looking for efficient ways to do that.

> **Janine Carlock encourages** her students to work independently, but her place in the front of the room does not mean she's not monitoring their work. She writes, "Occasionally I'll sit with a group, but I don't like to spend too much time with one group as I feel I'm not managing the class then. If I want them to work with each other only, I will stay up front. Often I write some vocabulary on the board that I hear students having trouble with or that is good for the whole class to learn. Sometimes I'll prep for the next class as I get ideas from the group work about what might be useful to work on next."

Ensuring Participation in Groups

As we show in Chapter 9, some students can be reluctant to work in groups. Students have many (valid) reasons for this, and teachers who have taught for a while are aware of this reluctance. For example, Jane Stanga notes, "I have seen some students who are reluctant to work in groups. It may be that they have had previous negative experiences in groups or they feel the pace of the group is too slow." And DeAnna Coon suggests, "I think a lot of it is personality, as well as cultural and/or language barriers. Some students are not accustomed to group work in their educational cultures; others want to work only with those of their native language group. Some are just more independent learners and would rather figure it out themselves, or perhaps they just find their classmates annoying." Allyson Noble also adds, "They don't trust others to be responsible for their part." Mary Charleza echoes this when she writes, "They might be afraid that others will make them do all the work."

In addition, some students who come from cultures in which men and women don't study side by side are often reluctant to work in groups with members of the opposite sex. In particular, women tend to be reluctant to work with men. Samantha Parkes notes that "female students from Middle Eastern countries often resist being paired with male students in the lower levels." She notes that this becomes problematic when there are just a few women in the class who wind up working with each other again and again.

Teachers would rather have students get over their reluctance rather than giving in to it. The alternative to using groups is a teacher-centered class, allowing students to work independently or just with the teacher. This would result in a quiet class in which very little communication or collaboration occurs. As Peter Ruffner notes, "Group work allows students to do more thinking in English and use their English more actively than they do when the teacher is leading the class."

> **Jane Stanga anticipates** that students may be unfamiliar with—and perhaps uncomfortable with—working in groups. She writes, "Early in the semester, I lead a discussion of the pros and cons of group work. This gives me an idea of general attitudes about group work among a particular class of students. We look at the con list and I have them brainstorm on things they can do if something they don't like occurs in a group. This process might need to be repeated again later in the semester, but I think it helps a lot to set the tone early that they have some power to change things they don't like."

Since language can't develop if it's not used for communication and in collaboration, teachers manage groups in a variety of ways to help students overcome their hesitations. Once students get the hang of it, they are much more effective participants in their groups. In fact,

Samantha Parkes adds that once the Middle Eastern women who are often reluctant to work in groups have been in her program for a while and are at a higher level, they seem to be more willing to work in a group with men.

As shown in this chapter, 96 percent of teachers report that they walk from group to group while their students are working (see Figure 15). In classrooms where groups are not functioning well, teachers have to do more than walk around to check that everyone understands and is on task. One strategy to make students more comfortable working in groups is to join the group. Instead of standing above the students, teachers sit down in the group. A female teacher in particular can sit in a group between a man and woman who are reluctant to work together. She doesn't have to sit very close to the man; she can model how to interact from a moderate distance.

DeAnna Coon writes about sitting down with a group that is not working well: "I monitor the groups and insert myself briefly to get the interaction going if necessary. If they direct all of their interactions to me, I encourage them to talk to their group members, not me." A little role-playing can also help. If I have a group that is not functioning well, I sit down with the group and take on the role of one of the students. Perhaps I'm the one who is writing. I may deliberately make a mistake to encourage some correction and peer teaching. Or if another student is writing, I may ask that student to show me the paper, and I will model by saying, "I think you got the first one right, but I'm not sure about the second one. Fatima [other group member], what do you think about the second one?" Such modeling is also a good way to show the value of group work as a learning experience and not simply a way to get an exercise done.

Sometimes, as Allyson Noble notes, students need "strategies about how to express concerns, assign roles, and deal with different personalities in a polite and professional way." Most teachers, when setting up the group task, will either assign roles or have the group choose roles. If I have a group that is doing some vocabulary work with a novel, for example, I'll suggest that they need the handout, a pencil, a dictionary, and at least one copy of the novel. Then I'll say, "Decide who is going to be in charge of finding the word in the novel, who is going to be using the dictionary, and who is doing your writing. I'll be by in a minute to see which role each group member has chosen."

When group work or "cooperative learning" was a new concept 30 years ago, much was made of group roles. We had the leader, the recorder, the timekeeper, the spokesperson, and so on. It seems that group work, at least in the ESL context, has evolved. Now the roles tend to grow somewhat organically out of the task. Sometimes teachers assign roles, and sometimes we ask students to divide up the work.

> **Celia Leckey notes** that if groups aren't working well together, the teacher can collaborate to help things along: "I will personally join any group where there is an issue and help them get through the exercise."

When I assign roles, I usually tell students why I am assigning those roles. For example, if time is running out at the end of the class, I might appoint the fastest writer to do the writing. Other times I take the pencil and paper away from the quiet student and ask that student to do more of the talking. And other times a student who struggles with accuracy has to do the writing while the other members check and cheer him on. As Elisabeth Chan writes, "Sometimes when I do group work, I make it part of the work to praise each other's answers. Or if I assign jobs within a group, one person is the 'cheerleader,' and it's his/her job to say 'good job' after each answer."

We have also seen that students may be reluctant to work in groups because they are afraid that their group mates may not pull their weight, which usually causes teachers to step in. Antonina Rodgers writes, "The biggest issue has been unreliable partners who leave most of the work to other members of the group." When this happens, she lets the students know that she is aware that one member of the group didn't contribute enough, and she tells that student, "You haven't contributed adequately to your group effort. You will have another chance to show that you can be an equal contributor."

When group work involves out-of-class work, such as when students are preparing a group presentation, teachers can foster good communication strategies. Group projects are all the rage in college and university courses, and virtually all require out-of-class prep time. ESL classes are a safe place to get some experience with this. When I form groups for this

10 Managing Student Interactions

kind of assignment, I usually give the groups ten or fifteen minutes at the end of class to talk about how they are going to communicate outside of class. They often talk about their class and work schedules and exchange email addresses and phone numbers.

> Elisabeth Chan has one more requirement when her students are preparing speeches in groups or pairs: "I tell the students that they have to cc me on every email about their project." This was useful recently when one member of a pair reported that his partner hadn't done any of the work; the partner simply read the PowerPoint slides that the student had prepared. Elisabeth was able to tell him that she believed him since she noted the partner had not replied to any emails.

Turn-taking may also be an issue when students are unfamiliar with working in groups. Stronger or more confident students may dominate, for example. Or, cultural norms may come into play, and older students may participate more than younger students. Teachers usually indicate in their instructions that students are to take turns. I often model this with one student or group, as back-and-forth or around-the-circle sometimes seem to be foreign concepts to some of my students.

There are also a few easy techniques that you can use to ensure participation by all. If students are collecting ideas in a brainstorm and you want everyone to contribute a few, give each student three or four poker chips (or something similar, like playing cards). Each time a student contributes an idea, she puts a poker chip into the middle of the group. Once a student's poker chips are gone, she should encourage her group-mates to talk, and everyone has to contribute until all of the poker chips are used up.

Similarly, if you want everyone to contribute to the writing of something, give everyone in the group a different color pen or pencil. I have a big box of colored pencils that I take to class for this technique. A colorful paper means everyone contributed! Students can also mark an article or sample essay in different colors (thesis = green, topic sentences = pink, concluding sentences = blue, and so on). Again, giving each student a different color—pencils or highlighters both work for this—forces collaboration when students might not be willing or able to collaborate without the teacher's direction.

Moving around the Room

As previously mentioned, a student-centered ESL class can look a lot like a traditional teacher-centered class at times—with students listening to an explanation or working quietly and individually on a piece of writing or a test. However, at other times, a student-centered ESL class looks nothing like a traditional class. One of those times is when students are out of their seats moving around the room.

> "In a collaborative classroom environment, students will move around more freely than in the traditional teacher-centered classroom."
>
> *Tom Hilanto*

While most teachers point out that their students do move around the classroom for a variety of reasons, teachers seem to have different comfort levels when it comes to having students up and around (see Figure 16).

I expect my students to feel free to occupy all parts of my classroom, and for this reason my first-week icebreaker usually asks them to stand up and move around the room. In my opinion, students need to own the classroom space to learn comfortably. Suzanne Mele Szwarcewicz echoes this, encouraging students to move even when not directed to move by her. She tells students "to find a good spot to work independently or to make a good decision if they are being distracted by others sitting near them."

As with other management issues, teachers seem to fall along a continuum when it comes to having students move around in their classrooms, and they have well-thought-out reasons for doing what they do. On one end of the continuum are teachers who rarely ask students to get out of their seats. John Politte points out that in his 90-minute classes, "I try to mimic a real, academic classroom because most of my students

10 Managing Student Interactions 123

Figure 16

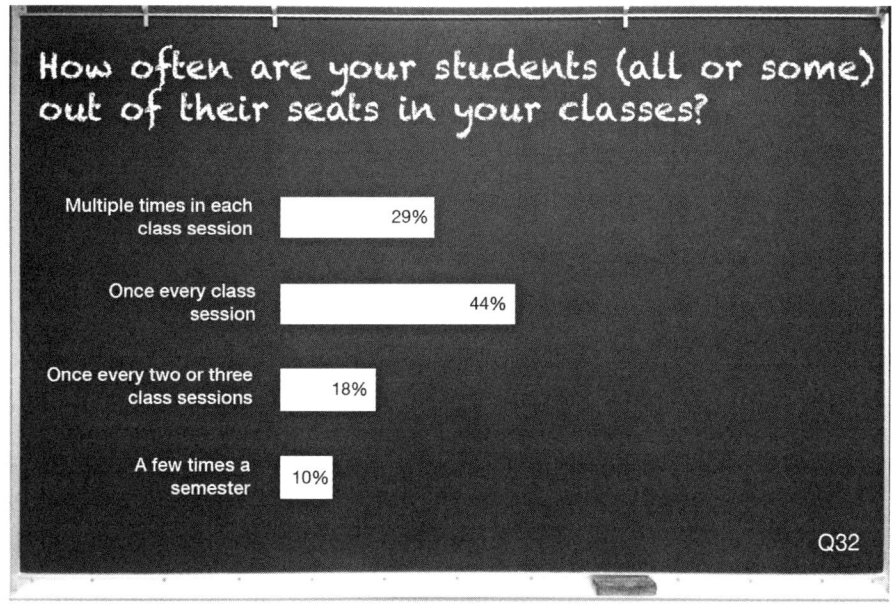

Note: Additional responses to this item appear in Appendix 3.

will enter academic classrooms after my class. When they are making presentations, they are out of their seats, but otherwise not."

Other teachers are more deliberate about building movement into their lesson plans. Therese Kravetz points out that "standing is better for the brain and body than sitting; I always get students up out of their seats." And Wendy Asplin notes, "This is critical. I teach 2.5-hour classes. Having students get out of their seats keeps them from getting sleepy." Allyson Noble characterizes this as a "good brain break!" (see Figure 17).

> "During long class sessions, I encourage my students to get out of their seats at least once. In short classes, they may just move their desks together for group work."
>
> *Kathleen Wax*

Many teachers ask students to move around the room to form groups (see Figure 17). As we have seen, teachers often ask students to form groups with their "neighbors" in the classroom, especially when

Figure 17

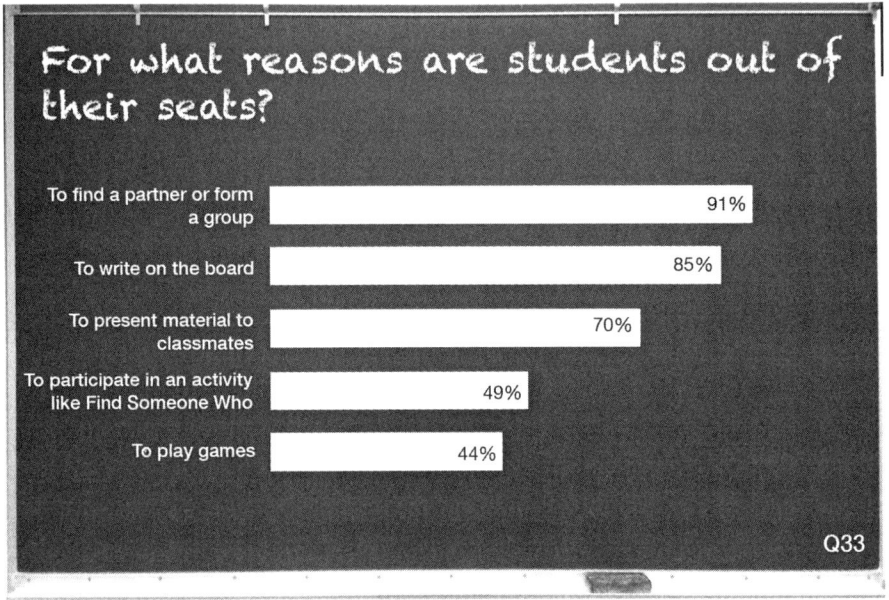

Note: Respondents checked more than one response; totals do not add up to 100 percent. Additional responses to this item appear in Appendix 3.

time is short, but other times we want to mix it up a little. We may want the people who always choose seats in the back of the room to move closer to the front, so we orchestrate some kind of whole-class shuffle. I tend to do this when my class seems tired or bored, or when pockets of students seem too comfortable or too uncomfortable with each other. A few minutes up and walking to form new groups or pairs energizes the class a little.

Teachers also ask students to stand up to write on the board (see Figure 17). This is, in fact, a hallmark of student-centered classes as there is something symbolic about putting the chalk or markers in the students' hands. In a teacher-centered class, the teacher may be seen as the holder and conveyer of knowledge, and she holds the chalk. In a student-centered class, responsibility for learning is shared, and so is the chalk!

Many teachers have students write answers or responses to exercises on the board. Students can do this in pairs or teams if they are reluctant to stand up alone—ask one student to hold the textbook and the other to do the writing. If I just want to get an exercise checked to

10 Managing Student Interactions

move on to something else quickly, I motivate the students to stand up and move to the board by advising them, "If you go first, you get to choose the one that you do! Go do an easy one!" Those students then get to give the marker or chalk to a classmate, so I'm not tasked with getting the reluctant students out of their seats—their peers are. Other times I move through the class and hand out chalk or markers—enough to make the board area comfortably crowded but not gridlocked. I usually choose my more confident students to go up first, and I tell them to choose who gets the chalk next.

> **Stephanie Sareeram has a very** participatory class environment. She writes, "I get students up at least once if not twice a class. I have them do a lot of board writing to workshop pieces of their work (thesis statements, main idea sentences, titles, topic sentences) or check their work from exercises. This allows for full-class collaboration—they love correcting each other—as well as for having copious examples of one thing. Having 25 thesis statements, all from the class, makes for a lot of samples and shows there is more than one way to write something."

Of course some skill areas and levels lend themselves to more movement in the classroom. In an oral communication class, students not only stand up for presentations but for other interactive activities. A running dictation is a good example of this: Students are situated in groups, and some information that they need is posted on the classroom walls. A representative from each group runs to the wall, has a look, and returns to report to the group, where the information is written down by a different group member.

When we work on questions in my lower-level classes, students are often out of their seats. Yes-no questions can be practiced by playing Twenty Questions, as long as the students have enough vocabulary. I'll never forget the time, in my first year of teaching, when a student from Cambodia was at the board leading Twenty Questions. It turned out that he didn't know the name of the animal that he was thinking of in

English. In fact, he'd never seen this animal out of Cambodia. So when the class "lost" the game and he had to divulge the answer, he turned to the board and drew a stick figure of something with four legs, a head, and a tail. The class had a good laugh, and this novice teacher learned a lesson about pre-teaching vocabulary before an activity!

> **Dorothy Gudgel points out** that in lower levels, students are more likely to be participating in Find Someone Who and similar activities. She has students out of their seats "more in the beginning-level classes—for information grids, for example."

Another fun interactive activity for yes-no questions is Who Am I? In this activity, I tape the name of a famous person to each student's back, and they circulate around the room asking only yes-no questions to figure out who they are. You can use the names of living people if you are only working in present tense, historical figures if you are working in past tense, or mix it up for a higher-level class. It is essential, especially with lower levels, to model this several times before students get out of their seats. To model, I stick a name to my own back and pretend that I don't know what it is (or have students choose a card from a stack to tape to my back, and then I really don't know!), and students answer my yes-no questions until I guess the name. Then one brave student comes to the front to repeat that process in front of the group and another if necessary. Once I'm sure everyone knows what to do, we can start the activity. The tricky part of this is to be sure everyone **knows** the famous people. Also, you'll have to judge how comfortable your students are with being someone of the opposite gender. If I do that, I generally model with a man's name on my back ("Am I am man?" "Yes, you are." "Ah, so just for today I am a man! Interesting.") I often also let the class choose a card to put on my back so I can participate. They can choose from some leftover cards, or write one themselves as I step out of the room for a minute. If I participate, I'm modeling correct question-and-answer forms in the middle of the pack of students and can gently prod those within earshot for accuracy.

10 Managing Student Interactions

I also like to get students out of their seats to put something in order. This may be a whole-class activity or a group activity. For example, I have often taught poems in my oral communication classes. Once I've done several activities with a poem, I cut it up, hand each student a line or a stanza, and they put themselves in order across the front of the room or in a semi-circle. They refer to the complete poem in their book or on a handout if they haven't memorized it. I've used parts of Longfellow's "Paul Revere's Ride" as well as Poe's "Annabel Lee" for this activity. Recently I filmed the group reading "Annabel Lee" by standing in the middle of the semi-circle with my tablet. I uploaded the recording to our private YouTube channel for the students to view at home.

As was mentioned in Unit Two, once I have my students learn an activity, I usually like to do a similar activity a few times. So the class who stood up to read "Annabel Lee" did the same activity later in the semester with a folk tale. We followed the same procedure: They read the story at home, listened to me read it several times, and listened to it on a recording. Then I cut it into paragraphs, they stood up and put themselves in order (referring to their book as needed), practiced with a partner, and practiced once as a whole class. During both practices I intervened with gentle corrections on their pronunciation and intonation. Then I filmed them, uploaded it to YouTube, and asked them to watch and analyze it for homework.

In my higher-level composition class, I have an ordering activity that I do in large groups. My students have to learn how to integrate a quote into an essay following MLA style. I type sentences using a huge font and print them on sheets in the landscape layout. (You can also write them on sentence strips you buy at a teacher supply store.) Each group gets a sentence. If I have 24 students, I may have four groups of six students each, so I cut each sentence into six pieces. Some pieces are just punctuation marks, as they are the tricky bits. Each group gets a turn to stand up and show their sentence to the rest of the class by holding the sheets up. The rest of the class gives a thumbs-up if the group gets it right.

Finally, my students stand when we play a game. For example, I play an end-of-novel game in my reading classes in which groups have to identify quotes from the novel. The groups each choose a novel-related name, such as the name of a character or group of characters. They write their group names on the board. To play the game, each group picks a quote out of a bag, has a few minutes to identify it, and sends a representative up to the document camera to present it. A panel of judges decides if the group gets full or partial credit, and a score-keeper keeps track of each group's points on the board. Except for passing through the class when the groups are ready for a new quote, I sit on the sidelines and let the class run the game. I usually print up enough quotes for four or five rounds, so that each member of the group can come up at least once.

> **Elizabeth Rasmussen notes** that she has her students out of their seats "to manipulate something, like putting pieces of an essay in order. This is easier if the students are standing around one desk."

Of course, I always encourage my students to stand when standing makes sense. If a group of three students is working to put story strips into order, it makes sense for one or two of them to stand up so that all three can read the strips. If a group finishes an exercise first, it makes sense for that group to go to the board and write the answers. My students also stand to bring their group's completed work up to the document camera, and often stay by the camera to present their work. If students are working independently or in small groups, I often invite them to use the online dictionary on the classroom computer. No one should feel shy about walking in my room (except perhaps to use the pencil sharpener when I'm talking!).

Finally, some teachers encourage students to get up and move on a class break. Nina Liakos points out, "I think it's good for students to get up occasionally. I make sure we take regular breaks—2 for every 3-hour block." Sometimes I teach longer classes that meet for four or five hours on one day. In those classes, I insist that we take a break and urge students to stand up and leave the room during the break. I can understand that students and teachers alike might want to skip the break and end class 20 minutes early. However, when I took some one-day-a-week graduate courses recently, I realized that one's brain really does stop working after a few hours. I find that we get more accomplished after the students come back from break than if I'd just powered through.

10 Managing Student Interactions

> Jim Toepper teaches a reading class that meets for five hours once a week. He writes, "I tried shorter breaks for the first 2 sessions with bad results. Each fifteen-minute break lasted about 20. Since then I've given a half-hour break with much better results. I don't require that they move around, but it seems most if not all are up before I leave the room. Many seem to bring food while others go to the cafeteria for coffee or other liquids. I also have them do a good amount of moving/shifting/finding a newly assigned partner during classroom activities. If they were to sit for five hours, I'd be tired *for* them."

Students may be out of their seats to give them a break from learning or because being up and around is what they need to accomplish a task or focus on a particular language feature. While it may feel like a natural flow to our students, this is one of many examples of how teachers manage the movement in their classrooms. Whatever the situation, teachers make decisions, often on the spot, about how to manage student interactions in groups, about when to intervene and when to let students figure it out, and about how to give students ownership of the learning space.

Chapter 11
Discussion in the Student-Centered Classroom

While pair and group work is at the heart of student-centered learning, there is still a place for whole-class discussions in many kinds of ESL classes. We work hard to create community and to make sure that students know each other, and sometimes students appreciate the chance to interact with everyone. This chapter discusses how teachers lead whole-class discussions and offers opinions and advice about bringing controversial topics into the classroom.

Whole-Class Discussions

I have previously mentioned that I was an early adopter of using groups in my ESL classes. In my classes, everything can be—and often is—group work. In fact, I find that I may in some cases over-use group discussion at the expense of whole-class interaction. Some years ago I visited a class and observed a beautifully managed whole-class discussion of the end of a novel. That was when I realized that I needed to use this technique more. The students had struggled, as a class, through the reading of the novel, and I could see that they appreciated this whole-class time to reflect as a group on the sad ending that the novel presented.

From the class I observed, I realized that there is an art to leading a whole-class discussion. Just as teachers make a conscious choice about where to be when they present material, they make equally thought-out but different choices about where to place themselves in the room for a whole-class discussion (see Figure 18).

I am again in the minority, agreeing with 33 percent of participants who like to sit on the teacher's desk at least occasionally when leading a discussion (see Figure 18). I feel that this lends a sense of informality to the class that I don't usually have, and it also allows me to see everyone clearly and not block anyone's view of a classmate. I think that, by

Figure 18

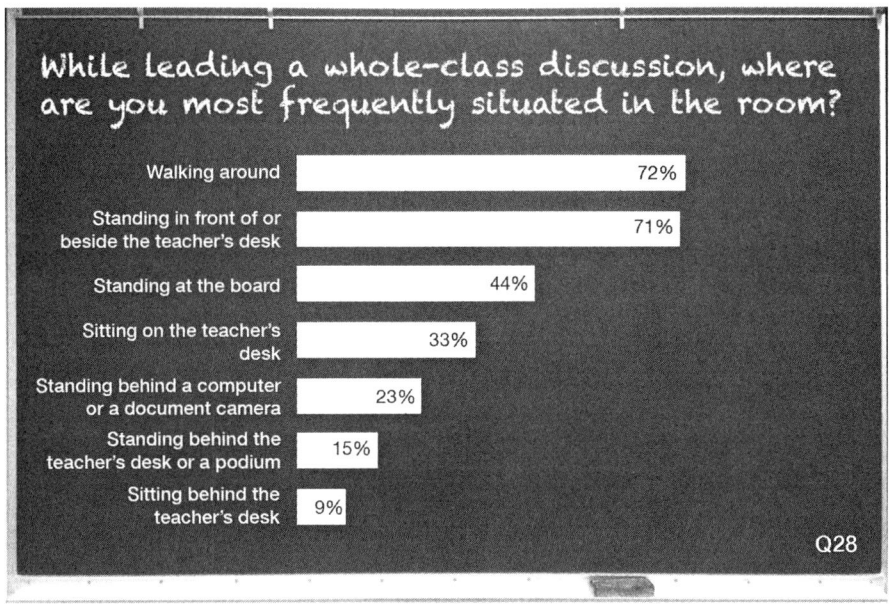

Note: Respondents checked more than one response; totals do not add up to 100 percent.

sitting, I am showing the students that we are talking for the sake of talk and not as part of a lesson. Peter Ruffner describes his decision to sit on the desk this way: "Sometimes it feels right to project the image of a relaxed participant in the conversation, to make it feel less like an academic exercise and more like an informal discussion. I've noticed that this often leads students to relax and feel free to express their views without worrying so much about being right or wrong."

Others achieve this relaxed atmosphere by sitting down with the students. Janine Carlock prefers to sit with the students in a circle. She writes, "I usually form a circle and sit in one of the student desks as part of the circle. I like to create a sense of 'us' as a class, with the teacher included, for group discussion. I lead the discussion, but they should do most of the talking."

On the survey, 72 percent of respondents report walking around the room during discussions (see Figure 18). Teachers who choose to move around while leading a whole-class discussion have similarly well-thought-out reasons for doing so. Karen Vlaskamp notes that "by walking around (a little), I feel conversation is easier when I close the gap between the student talking and me." And Riley Holzberlein notes, "I feel more engaged with the class being out from behind the desk." Nigel Caplan says, "My engagement encourages theirs, I believe."

> "Your body language should give an impression of being involved and somewhat more equal with the students to encourage participation during discussions."
>
> *Megan Calvert*

While in some cases teachers see themselves as leading the discussion, many teachers see themselves as creating the opportunity for discussion without leading it. Darlene Branges comments, "If I walk around, then they don't see me as the 'leader' of the discussion." Samantha Parkes takes herself out of the discussion. She explains, "I sometimes stand to the side of the room so students can make eye contact with each other." And Stephen Lewis writes, "I like to walk around to bring the conversation to the individual who is speaking."

> "Ideally, the desks would be in a circle and I would be seated as the students are. By standing, I feel like I'd be presenting myself as the authority figure and run the risk of either controlling the discussion or intimidating students who are physically 'lower' than me."
>
> *Gregory Kennerly*

Recording Ideas During Discussion

In many classes, discussions are brainstorms to collect ideas for writing or another class assignment. In that case, teachers often locate themselves at the board or near a document camera. In fact, 44 percent of teachers may be standing at the board during a discussion (see Figure 18). Stephanie Sareeram notes that "being by the board allows me to write their ideas up quickly or clarify a point easily." This is the case in my classes as well. I may start the discussion informally, perched on the teacher's desk, but as soon as we start to float a lot of ideas, I run to the board or document camera to start some kind of graphic organizer. Unfortunately, that is also when my students reach for their pens as well. That's when I beg them not to write and promise to share my notes. While I often encourage my students to take notes during class, if the focus is on generating ideas then I think it is better if the students just talk and let me do the writing.

If I write on a sheet of paper on the document camera, I can photocopy that for everyone or scan it, create a PDF, and post it online. If I write on a blackboard or whiteboard, recently I've been taking a picture of the board with my phone or tablet and posting that. In a later class, I can project the saved image on the screen while they are drafting a composition, for example.

> **Janice Hornyak captures** the flow of her class this way: "During whole-class discussion, I might sit on the desk, but I would usually be moving around, and at some point I'd probably be running over to the board or document camera as we make our lists or sum things up."

During this part of my class, I may be talking a lot. I generally don't add my ideas to the discussion, but I tend to repeat what students say as I make notes. Perhaps this is a holdover from my training in the audiolingual method when teachers were urged to repeat a "correct utterance" after students spoke. But I do think it's useful, especially at lower levels when students can't understand each other easily, or in larger rooms where they can't hear each other well. When I have the chance to visit a class, sometimes I notice that when the teacher doesn't repeat what is said, the other students are clearly not following the discussion. So I repeat for that reason and also to recap our discussion so far to allow for some thinking about where the discussion is going. In addition, if students are to use the ideas from the discussion in writing, I want them to have heard the ideas several times before they start to write. Again, this is perhaps more relevant in lower levels than in higher academic ESL classes.

Controversial Topics

Most of the teachers surveyed for this book teach adults or young adults, many in college or university settings. While many college classes, seminars, and campus events deal with controversial issues, the question is, Does discussing and writing about controversial topics promote or hinder learning? What do teachers have to keep in mind while approaching potentially sensitive topics? (See Figure 19.)

> "People have different ideas on what is controversial. I like to bring up topics that are of interest to the students and are creative and inspirational."
>
> *Therese Kravetz*

Many teachers deal with controversial topics if they come up, but they don't go out of their way to inject controversy into the classroom. For example, Samantha Parkes writes, "I cover the syllabus, which may or may not have 'controversial' topics, but this is a subjective term (and

Figure 19

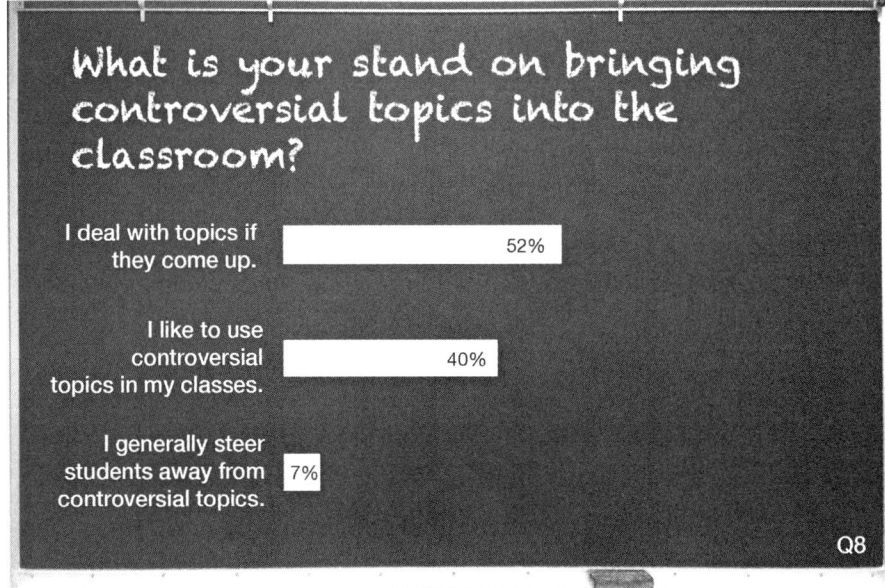

cultural). I don't organize my class around them, but don't avoid them either. If the topic is timely, we discuss it, but I don't have classes focused on taboos of conversation in American culture like religion, abortion, gun rights, etc."

With any group of students, it would be difficult to have any kind of interesting discussion while avoiding controversy completely. As Tom Hilanto points out, "In reality, a mixed ESL classroom will always contain controversial topics because of cross-cultural differences. What is controversial in one culture is often a norm in another. One example of this is pre-marital dating." In other words, any use of current issues is sure to bring controversy of one sort or another. Even our textbooks may unwittingly inject controversy, and we have to acknowledge that our students view these topics as controversial. Stephanie Sareeram explains, "When topics come out of the blue from student discussion—such as when a student who does not believe in evolution objects to the primates unit in our textbook—I try to show that I respect the student's opinion but that the course content supports a differing theory/viewpoint."

> **Sherlie Scribner writes** about controversial topics, many of which appear in our textbooks, in the context of her students' cultural backgrounds: "Some of the controversial topics that we consider conversation-worthy are irrelevant to our students. If they come from a country that doesn't allow guns, they aren't really interested in gun control debates. I try to explain other concepts in value-neutral terms. An example is single mothers who have never been married. Some of my students have a difficult time understanding this concept, but it is included in the course textbook."

Scaffolding Controversial Topics

When teachers bring controversial topics to their classes for discussion, they are often careful to provide the support and scaffolding needed to make it a successful experience for the class. Later on, when our students are integrated into college classes or perhaps debating coworkers around the water cooler, they'll have the skills that we give them to fall back on. First and foremost, we can alert students to topics we consider to be taboo in polite conversation. As Nataliya Schetchikova explains, "I stay away from topics related to politics, religion, and sexual orientation in the classroom. Most other topics are healthy for students—they need to learn to discuss controversial topics in a respectful manner."

Students may need to be taught some phrases to use to politely disagree, for example. We can teach students to say, "I understand your point of view. However, . . ." In my advanced composition class, I have students memorize transitions like *Not everyone agrees with me. Some people believe . . .* and *What these people don't take into consideration is. . .* And, of course, supporting with facts rather than emotion takes a lot of energy and critical thinking. It's hard enough in one's first language!

> "My class is called 'Contemporary/Controversial Topics,' so we have 'the talk' at the beginning about how to discuss differences respectfully. We discuss/debate just about anything, and I always moderate, but I've never had a problem."
>
> *John Politte*

In general, teachers like to bring up controversial topics in higher-level classes more often than in lower levels, where students may lack the vocabulary to argue effectively. Even at higher levels, it is useful to pre-teach some vocabulary related to the issue at hand. Teachers also gauge the personality of the class before introducing such topics. Leslie Sheen describes her approach: "I like to use controversial topics at the higher levels when I know the students have the vocabulary to cope with the discussion. I also wait a few weeks to get a feel for the class's receptivity to such topics. If I feel that students have a good level of respect for one another and for me, then I will proceed with the controversial topics because they often allow for natural use of language as well as helping to pique the interest and motivation of many students."

Kay Marshall seems to concur. She explains, "I try to be careful with this, especially in the first part of the semester before the students

11 Discussion in the Classroom

know each other. I've gotten into a couple of sticky situations where, for example, students have (unwittingly) used insulting language based on stereotypes. In speaking and listening classes, though, they learn debating and persuasive speaking skills, so here I have effective and 'controlled' ways to teach them about this."

In fact, as previously mentioned, teachers have effective ways to scaffold the experience of dealing with controversial topics. I like to use a "human Likert scale" to get students out of their seats to "vote with their feet" on occasion with a controversial issue. Students arrange themselves along a continuum from Strongly Agree to Strongly Disagree or move into different corners of the room. This helps to show students that someone they like and respect can have a different opinion. This is often a very good first lesson in a unit on persuasive writing or debate.

> **Megan Calvert explains** how she uses a human Likert scale: "I might give the students a sentence such as 'Technology makes our lives better' and then indicate to them an invisible line in a long, empty space in the classroom and where to stand along the line if they strongly agree, somewhat agree, somewhat disagree, or strongly disagree. Students then move to the appropriate space as they decide and commit to opinions. This hopefully leads to a short discussion in which students explain and defend their views. I also encourage students to move if they change their opinions as the discussion progresses, as one side coaxes people over from the other. This helps reinforce the idea that opinions don't need to be static."

It's also a good idea to let students read and think about a topic before asking them to discuss it. Jane Stanga describes using controversial topics with her classes: "I have set up debates in which students have to research the pros and cons of a topic and come to class prepared to argue either side. I have done this with the pros and cons of microcredit, cohabitation outside of marriage, and human rights versus animal rights. I believe a more structured approach avoids an opinion-based argument." Asking students to be prepared to support both sides of the argument is very good for their critical thinking.

> "If a topic is very controversial, I prefer if it's part of a writing assignment so the students can make their case without worrying about others' reactions. In a discussion, students should use rules about how to disagree politely and still make their case. It's the teacher's responsibility to take control of the situation if things get out of hand."
>
> *Mary Charleza*

It is certainly possible to bring in controversial topics while avoiding cultural taboos or emotionally charged issues. When I use such "white bread" controversial topics, I often randomly assign students sides in the argument to force them to see both sides. Some that I have used recently include topics from the news as well as ones related to my college:

- Should cities install red-light cameras at busy intersections?
- Should teachers receive bonuses if their students do better than average on standardized tests?
- Is a college education really worth it?
- Is it a good idea to take a "gap year" between high school and college?
- Should our community college build and operate a dorm?
- Should parking fees be eliminated at our college?

My students never know my opinion on these topics. Elizabeth Whisnant echoes that: "I tend not to make my personal views known, but rather draw out students' opinions and offer them alternative points of view if necessary."

Teachers clearly wear many hats when it comes to whole-class discussions in their student-centered classrooms. They are at times facilitators, moderators, or participants. They are summarizers and recorder of ideas. And they are scaffolders and—of course—**teachers** as they introduce students to the nature of discussion in American classrooms.

Classroom Interactions: Wrap-Up

I am probably not the only ESL teacher in my community college who has had a visit from a teacher in a neighboring room—never another ESL teacher, of course!—asking us to keep the noise down. My students might be dragging desks into a new configuration, working in groups to create Venn diagrams on large sheets of paper, or dashing to the board to be the first to complete an exercise, all resulting in more noise than any teacher-centered class will ever generate.

What probably upsets my neighbor even more is that she doesn't see me at the front of the room lecturing when she comes in to talk with me. In fact, I'm often sitting with a group of students, or I might be behind the computer preparing the next part of class while my students debate something in their groups. I'm sure she thinks my class is chaos, but if we have the chance to talk, I can explain exactly why everything is happening. I am indeed managing classroom interactions.

Yes, my students are often quietly listening to me, writing, or collaborating. I'd like to remind my neighbor of that and reassure her that the noisy part of our class won't last too long. Language is only language when it's used for communication, and sometimes communication gets noisy. ESL teachers know this, and manage it in their classrooms in a variety of ways to allow it to happen.

Making Connections

Challenging Beliefs: What Teachers Think

What's your opinion? Circle the extent to which you agree or disagree with this statement. To read survey responses to the statement, please turn to Appendix 1 (pages 181–183).

> It's a good idea to bring jokes and humor into the classroom.
>
> strongly agree   agree   neither agree nor disagree   disagree   strongly disagree

Classroom Connections: What Teachers Do

In a class you are teaching or visiting, you may want to consider some of these points about how the classroom space and talk are managed.

1. Is there teacher-led direct instruction? If so, where is the teacher during this part of the class?

2. How is the blackboard or whiteboard used during the class?

3. Are questions used in direct instruction?

4. Are modeling or think-alouds used? Is the instruction scaffolded? Note that if you are visiting the class, this may not be evident unless you interview the teacher.

5. What is the teacher's role while students are working in groups? Where is the teacher during group-work time?

6. How is student participation in group work ensured?

7. Do students have roles while they are working in groups?

8. Are students out of their seats during the class session? If so, for what reason(s)?

9. Is there any whole-class discussion?

10. If controversial topics are used, how are they handled?

Strategies and Motivations: What Teachers Say

Consider these comments from survey respondents on a few of the topics from this unit.

On accommodating students' preferences regarding working in groups:

Teachers understand and even sometimes identify with students' reluctance to work in groups, and often even adjust how much group work they include based on the personality of the class.

Judy Snyder: "On the rare occasion that someone has complained to me, I have either asked the student to tell me which students he/she would like to work with (since group work is going to happen despite the student's preferences), or asked the student to be a good sport and 'play along' for a while because individual work will also be a part of the class."

Elaine George: "Sometimes I allow them to work alone. Other times, I give my 'You have to play the game' speech. Sometimes you have to do things you don't want to do in order to get paid (or get a grade)."

On getting students up and out of their seats during class or on breaks:

Many teachers understand that learning a language is hard work, and that sometimes our class sessions are quite long. They use movement as a strategy to keep the learning going.

Robyn Brinks Lockwood: "Simply put, it keeps them active and involved."

George A. Flowers: "I typically alternate between whole-class and group activities. Sometimes I have groups interacting with other groups. Sometimes I have students writing at the white board."

Elizabeth Rasmussen: "We go for two hours with no break, so I like to have my students move to a new group, or go to the boards, or do some physical activity in each class."

On using controversial topics to foster critical thinking:

Many teachers think that a good way to prepare students for U.S. college classrooms is by discussing, debating, and writing about controversial topics in the ESL classroom.

Dana Kappler: "Controversy means they are using critical-thinking skills, and since I teach in a college, I feel we should act like an academic institution."

DeAnna Coon: "Bringing these topics in often opens up new ways of thinking for students, which is essential to developing critical-thinking skills. I think avoiding them is a true disservice."

Megan Calvert: "I like to challenge students' ideas in a way that helps to increase tolerance and appreciation for diversity. You're already helping students to step outside their own cultural and linguistic boxes, so you're already challenging their world views on some level just by teaching them another language. A good language class, in my opinion, should open people's minds in multiple ways."

George A. Flowers: "I don't go out of my way to bring in controversial topics, but I frequently use controversy as a means of generating interaction. There are very few topics that haven't been addressed in my classroom at one time or another."

On exercising caution with controversial topics:

Many teachers report that they are somewhat conservative when it comes to using controversial topics in the classroom.

Nigel Caplan: "The goal of my class is to teach language, and controversy can get in the way of that unnecessarily. However, sometimes it's important to discuss a topic for the students to build cultural schema. I don't censor topics if students raise them."

Judy Snyder: "There are some topics that I've learned to avoid because they elicit such strong reactions from some students. This is true for an issue like abortion, for which the students' religious training and cultural background have often given them inflexible views. When I give my students the option to choose an essay or discussion topic, I always maintain veto power!"

Wendy Asplin: "This really depends on the course, and what is meant by controversial. Would I discuss women driving in Saudi Arabia? Probably not. Would I discuss same-sex marriage? Maybe, but only if it were on the ballot or if someone brought it up. There are plenty of ways to encourage critical thinking without going into topics that are uncomfortable (which I used to do when I was a younger teacher)."

Elaine George: "I teach students from many different cultures, political situations, and religions." She writes, "It is useless to 'debate' beliefs based in religion or culture, and this can cause hard feelings between students. I try to find 'interesting' topics rather than 'controversial' ones."

Unit Five:
Classroom Trouble Spots

Until now we have looked at ways to create a positive classroom environment, including setting the right tone and creating class rules that foster respect for time, space, and fellow learners. We've considered the use of students' first languages and involving the students in decisions about the use of their L1s. We've looked at lesson planning and student questions as well as integrating pair and group work into lessons. And, we've looked at managing the physical classroom space as well as the talk within that space.

Through all of these topics we see that at any given moment a teacher is juggling several dimensions and making many decisions, often on the spot, to maintain student-centered learning. However, sometimes no matter what we do to create a positive learning environment, we are met with trouble spots—incidents that interfere with the learning experience. Some of those may be caused or perhaps exacerbated by our programs, such as when they allow students to join the class late or when they schedule classes to begin at the height of rush hour. Some may be caused when student expectations collide with ours, such as when we must ask for cell phones to be turned off when they are hardly ever turned off nowadays. And some may be caused by cultures coming into contact, such as when we have to communicate that class begins at the published time and that late arrivals are frowned upon in American culture.

As with previous points in this book, the teachers surveyed have a wealth of well-considered advice to share on many of these trouble spots (see Figure 20). This unit shares many of them.

Chapter 12
Arrivals and Breaks

In Chapter 2, we saw that teachers' most important class rules are about respect, and some of that respect is for the time of the class. Indeed, when—for one reason or another—that time is not respected, this can turn into a class trouble spot. This chapter deals with students who come late or take unauthorized breaks.

Joining the Class Late

Some programs allow students to join classes late. They may have rolling registration for a couple of weeks, viewing this strategy as a way to serve their population by not excluding students who may not have known about the school's calendar. Programs may also try to accommodate

Figure 20

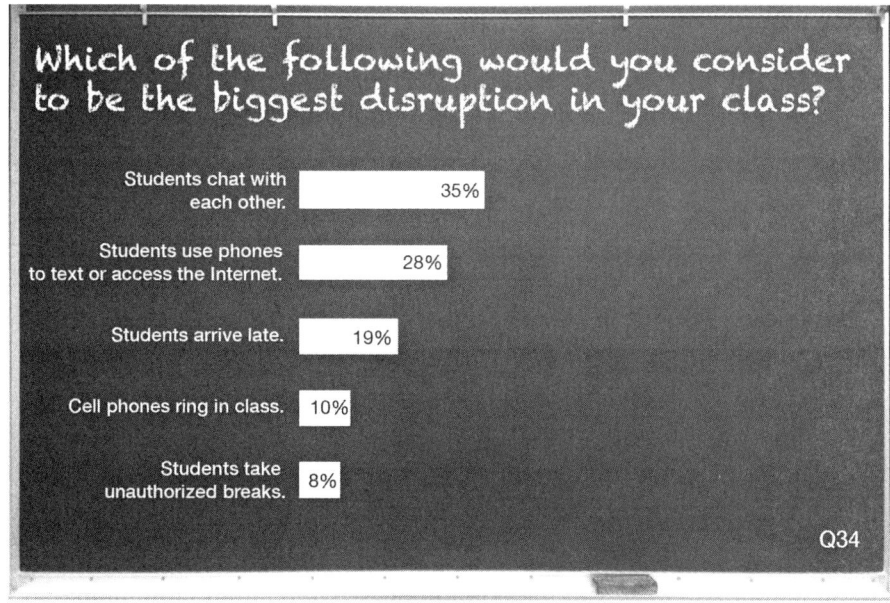

students' travel schedules, acknowledging that international travel over summer or winter holidays can be unpredictable.

Perhaps because of this relaxed policy, even students who register on time sometimes don't show up for the first meeting of the class. My students sometimes look at me in disbelief when I tell them, as a student, that I would never, for any reason, miss the first day of a class. In fact, our textbook includes a story written by a college student who has an accident with a cigarette lighter on her way to class and who attends the class smelling of singed hair. I ask my students if that surprises them, and they usually answer that it does, that they would have gone home to clean up instead of attending the class.

Not having everyone present on the first day of the session is quite problematic. Students who are present expect the course to begin on the first day, and teachers certainly want to use every possible instructional day. As George Flowers notes, "I start with real, productive assignments on Day One." He tries to ensure that his students are present on the first day: "I communicate with students via email two weeks in advance telling them that attendance will be required and that we will actually begin on the first day of class."

This strategy depends on, of course, students registering on time and checking the email account provided by the college or university. Even then, some students may choose to skip the first day. I have suspected that some weak students want to avoid the diagnostic testing that I do on the first day because they are afraid I might counsel them to move to a lower level. Or, some students may expect that we are going to go over the syllabus and do an icebreaker, and they'd rather just skip that. However, as previously noted, many of us get to some very productive assignments on the first day. I always remember the student(s) who join the class late and have them in some mental category throughout the semester, as they are often the ones who don't do well. Stephanie Sareeram has a direct approach with students who choose not to attend the first class: "If the student seems to have arrived late because he couldn't pay attention to the details of the start of classes, I usually lay down the law with that student so he knows more is expected of him than he's shown by this careless start."

In addition to the students who register late because the program allows it and students who choose to miss the first day of class, we have a third category of late arrivers: students who are moved from another

12 Arrivals and Breaks 147

level. Students learn at different rates, placement tests aren't always perfectly accurate, and sometimes quite a bit of time passes between the end of one session and the beginning of the next—time when students have many opportunities to improve their English skills. For these reasons, every program I have ever been associated with conducts diagnostic testing in the first class or two, moving students to the level that is a better fit if need be. What this means in many programs is that we are doing a dance: Getting some real instruction started while moving some students out and accepting some new ones from other levels.

We can work hard to make our students understand the importance of showing up on the first day, but as we have seen, sometimes this is out of our control. Experienced teachers, then, report several strategies to deal with late arrivers.

One lemonade-from-lemons point to keep in mind is that much of what you repeat for the new arrivals may be useful repetition for the students who have been with you all along. Any reiteration of class rules or explanation of routines might be understood better the second time. And I always remember an anecdote that a teacher told me many years ago (in the days before the Internet and online information). She wrote her name on the board for the new arrival and noticed half a dozen other students write it down. They'd probably been too nervous on the first day to catch her name.

> **Breana Bayraktar seems** to be most concerned with bringing new additions up to speed in the course: "I sit down with them and we develop a plan for how they will catch up with the concepts/work missed. I am usually less concerned with how welcome/integrated they feel. (Perhaps I should be more concerned!)"

As with other practices, teachers seem to fall along a continuum when it comes to integrating late arrivals. I fall at the minimalist side of the continuum. Perhaps I should do more to integrate a new student, especially if she is coming from a different level and didn't choose to miss the first few days of my class. But by class three or four, my mind is often well beyond "first day" activities. I probably do what Karen Van Horn does: "Very simply, I say, 'It's nice to have you.' I tell them where we are in instruction at the moment and invite them to join us." I also do what Wendy Asplin advises: "Just welcome them and put them into one of the groups. I don't think it requires anything additional. The burden is on me to get that week's (important) handouts to them." And on the topic of handouts, if students arrive several days late by choice—after appearing on my roster—there is a very good chance that I will not even have handouts for them, as I clean my book bag out into the recycling bin frequently. It's tough love, but anything really important is available online.

Other teachers are more concerned with integrating the new arrival into the community of learners. Judy Snyder writes, "I try to get the students into a group that has been functioning well or that I have perceived as being particularly friendly. I also give the student a quick lesson on how/where to find important class information so that they can catch up." And Elizabeth Rasmussen writes, "I make sure they introduce themselves to the class, and I pair them with a buddy of the same gender, especially if they're new to our program. I meet with them after their first class to check that they can access Blackboard, answer any questions, and explain what they need to do to catch up."

> **Zaimah Khan notes that** community-building doesn't end on the first day or two of class. She writes, "For social integration, I do icebreakers periodically throughout the semester, with one in the class immediately after the final class roster has been set."

Many teachers use the collaborative environment in their classroom to enlist the help of classmates to integrate latecomers. For example, Suzanne Mele Szwarcewicz writes, "I ask students to explain rules and procedures, and sometimes buddy up the new student with an empathetic student who can be a partner for the first few days." And Tracy Bain Chase explains, "In the first week, I'll place the student in a group with students who are patient and are more likely to explain whatever is needed."

Finally, many teachers report that they meet with late additions outside of class. Janice Hornyak notes, "I ask them to stay after class a few minutes on their first day to tell them what we've done so far and to see if they have questions." I have to confess to not being so accommodating—especially if I am running to my next class. But if I have more than a couple of late additions I try to end class ten minutes early one day to meet with all of them at once. The students who have been attending all along are usually exhausted by the third or fourth class session and welcome this little break.

Arriving Late for Class

Joining the class late is one issue—sometimes within the student's control, sometimes not. But when students arrive late for class, most teachers believe the student is at fault, and they take measures to encourage students to arrive on time.

When teachers were asked about the one biggest disruption to their classes, 20 percent responded that they thought the biggest disruption is when students arrive late (see Figure 20).

Of course, sometimes a late arrival is not the student's fault. Some programs schedule classes nearly back-to-back, with five or ten minutes between each. And in those programs, some teachers hold students over—seemingly unaware that the students have another class to get to. And of course, traffic and weather sometimes come into play. But most teachers, when presented this list of reasons or excuses, will ask, "Why can 15 of my students arrive on time under the same conditions, while 5 are consistently late?"

Many teachers take a direct approach to reducing tardiness. Robyn Brinks Lockwood writes, "I have a firm rule and I make it high stakes. Being more than 10 minutes late constitutes an absence." And Janine Sacramone explains, "I mark them late, let everyone know that I don't like it, and make sure students know that 4 times late equals one absence."

While I like the idea of keeping track of late arrivals, I know myself too well to believe I could actually do this. I don't even usually take attendance until the middle or end of class, when I often just do a quick count or shout, "Who's not here?" I am just too wrapped up in what's going on to stop and note a tardy arrival, so I try to rely more on natural consequences to trip up the latecomers. In other words, I try to motivate students to arrive on time for something important. Lori Ward also does this, explaining, "I give quizzes at the very beginning of class, and if a student is late, he can't take it." However, the last time I tried this, it didn't work. I had a student who was consistently 20 minutes late, so I decided to begin most classes with some kind of short quiz, which he missed over and over. He did not pass the class—not because of the string of zeroes under his quiz grades, but because his skills did not improve. I lost the battle *and* the war on that one. And the poor students who arrived on time had to do perhaps 10 more quizzes than in a normal semester, and I had to grade them all (poor me). Time for a new strategy.

> **DeAnna Coon captures** a strategy I often use as well: "I generally ignore the latecomers and leave it up to them to figure out what's going on, where the class is, and to catch up in hopes that they'll make a better effort to be on time—since I'm not going to compensate for their tardiness. I've tried giving short graded quizzes at the beginning of each class, but it didn't seem to have any effect. In short, it's a losing battle."

Sometimes the best way to deal with tardiness is to get the class working right away, in addition to the start-of-class quiz described. Allyson Noble explains several strategies: "Have something graded that is only offered during the first 5–10 minutes of class (such as a warm-up or a small quiz). Or collect homework only during the first 5–10 minutes (a homework folder that is put away 10 minutes into the class, for example)." Knowing that class begins with some very productive time, even if it's not high-stakes like a quiz, may make students more conscientious about being punctual. If not, however, and if some students come in the middle of an exercise or activity, it's best to quickly integrate the student. Say, "Welcome, Mariam, we are doing Exercise 2 on page 47." Or simply point to the instruction written on the board.

There is, however, another opposite strategy that I have employed. When I have a group that tends to struggle in for whatever reason—perhaps they are coming from another class that frequently runs over and need a few minutes to get some coffee, or the class begins at 8:00 AM or 5:30 PM and many students commute long distances—I adjust my class schedule so that the first 20 or 30 minutes are very flexible. I use a folder system, so all of the work that I have to return to the students is in a folder on my desk. Students know that they walk in, pick up their folder, take a seat, and begin to go through what I have for them, conferring with me as questions come up or using my dictionary. Most of my classes require lots of revision and editing—of writing as well as grammar or vocabulary exercises. The late students miss this quality time with me, but they aren't missing any real instruction or group work. Again, this is not every term, but it is a strategy that I bring in every once in a while.

> **Cathleen McCargo writes** about communicating to students the importance of arriving on time: "I explain that part of learning a language is understanding the cultural norms that accompany it. Therefore, I explain that being late to class is an unacceptable practice in the United States."

Taking Unauthorized Breaks

Even more than late arrivals, unauthorized breaks really get on my nerves! My class sessions may start up slowly, as I have indicated, with a short quiz or some independent work time, but once I'm in the flow of the class—whether I'm explaining something or I have students working on a task in groups—I get really irritated when a student simply stands up and walks out. I am somewhat in the minority, as roughly 10 percent of respondents indicated that this is the biggest disruption in their classes (see Figure 20). Perhaps their students don't do this.

I often teach one in a series of three classes that meet from 8:00 AM to 3:20 PM, with just two 10- or 20-minute breaks between the classes. So I should be more forgiving, but I'm not. I schedule my class "with the break at the end," so I expect my students' full attention for 2 hours and 10 minutes of a 2-hour-20-minute class. I often wonder if my relaxed and friendly style invites students to believe it's OK to take a break without asking.

One way I've dealt with this is by alerting students to the fact that if they **must** leave the room, then the time we are transitioning to group work or perhaps when they are working on some individual writing are the best times to run out for a few minutes. But this backfires as it seems that it encourages more breaks and really cuts into instructional time.

Peter Ruffner has recently dealt with this issue. He has the same schedule as I do—2-hour and 20-minute classes that we traditionally shorten by 10 minutes by putting the break at the end. He writes, "Last semester I started giving my students a short break in the middle of my classes, and it worked very well. After the first few classes, I was able to stop the stragglers from coming back late from the break. I take French classes now, and though I'm very motivated, I'm happy that my professor gives a mid-class break. I can recharge my batteries, make a call, or use the restroom, so I don't have to take an 'unauthorized' break."

In a student-centered class, the students' presence is paramount. Students may be able to slip in late, leave early, or miss entirely a teacher-centered lecture class. However, when engagement of and by the learners is the core of the class, students must be present in every class session, on time, and for the full session. Teachers know that they must overcome several obstacles, from their programs' schedules to their students' cultural norms, and they craft policies and procedures to achieve this.

Chapter 13
Chatting, Helping, Cheating?

Even when we have all of our students present in the classroom, some negative behaviors might interfere with the learning environment. Sometimes these behaviors are subtle, or they begin innocently and blossom into a problem, so even a teacher who sets the right tone and crafts good class rules at the start of a session may need to figure out how to deal with these trouble spots as the session progresses. This chapter deals with those times when we don't want our students to talk or collaborate.

Chatting with Neighbors

One problem I encountered recently was chatting in the back of the room. In fact, 35 percent of teachers responded that chatting disrupts their classes (see Figure 20). In my case, I had a more mature student who seemed to set herself up as alternate teacher, chatting both in Arabic and in English. When I called her on it, again and again, she apologized and explained she was just helping her neighbors because they'd asked her a question, etc. It seemed that no matter who her neighbors were, the chatting continued.

> Lauren Boone has experienced a problem with chatting. She explains, "The students are all Chinese and want to chat to each other or explain things in Chinese while I am talking or doing something with the class. I stop and say, 'Now say that in English,' or 'Now explain that to X in English.' Every once in a while I say, 'Why don't you guys leave the room to have this discussion.'"

Teachers have some strategies to deal with excessive chatting. Suzanne Mele Szwarcewicz writes that she uses "some gestures to signal that I am waiting to speak, or that we are trying to listen to others." She also suggests that we "remind students that there will be time to talk later when they are working in groups." Silence often gets the chatters' attention. Elizabeth Rasmussen writes, "I stop what I'm saying and look at the students who are talking. Within seconds, one of their classmates tells them to be quiet." This way, the classmates take responsibility for each other's action, rather than making the teacher the enforcer.

> "I ask chatting students if they have a question I can help them with or if they would like to share something with their classmates."
>
> Bill Woodard

Ruth Takushi is bothered by chatting, especially when another student has the floor. She writes, "I ask the speaker to pause for a moment and ask the chatting students to listen and show respect for their classmate. Then I apologize to the speaker for interrupting and ask them to continue."

Helping or Cheating?

As shown with the example of the Chinese students, students often chat to help each other. In a student-centered classroom, we foster this sense of support, of peer teaching, and of collaboration. Even if we don't want students chatting while others are talking or having a conversation in their first language, we really don't want to prohibit student-to-student communication if there is a good reason for it. The problem is, in a test situation the collaboration needs to stop. Of course, some quizzes can be "open mouth, open book" as Judy Snyder likes to call them. But at some point, we need to check to see each student's individual progress, and many of us use quizzes, tests, or in-class essays for that. Students who are new to the student-centered environment sometimes have a hard time seeing this, so we need to make a distinction between "helping" and "cheating."

Some teachers report little trouble with cheating, notably in programs with honor codes. Robyn Brinks Lockwood notes, "My university has a strict honor code. I'm not even allowed to be in the room when students take a test." I'm not sure how my students would act if I left the room during a test, although I frequently mention honor codes to them. I tell them in my first graduate program, even though we did not have an honor code, professors always left us alone with tests and no one ever cheated. They find this hard to believe, and I wonder how they fare when they go on to universities with honor codes. Do they rise to it, or do they cheat?

> **Vivian Leskes explains,** "I give an introductory talk about the attitude toward cheating in the U.S. as compared to other cultures."

I had an email from a former student recently. She'd been in my class during her first semester at my community college, and several years later she was getting ready to graduate and move on to a university. She said she was writing for one reason, and that was to share with me that she felt that cheating was out of control in many of the classes she'd taken after mine (not just ESL). So I wonder: When teachers report that they don't find cheating to be a problem, is it possible that they just don't detect it?

Teachers who are wary of cheating have a few strategies to ensure that students do their own work on tests. Jane Stanga reports, "Before a test or quiz, I have them move their desks farther apart so they 'have room to work.' Unfortunately, I found out the hard way during my first semester that I have to watch carefully during tests and quizzes."

I also use the "have room to work" line, usually with a little humor or a wink. I tell them that I want them to do their best, so if they need to stretch, they should be far enough not to hit a neighbor if they extend both arms. They know what I mean and usually laugh (probably while thinking up a different way to cheat!). I also tell them that I've seen it all so I'll be watching them. I tell them I learned the numbers in several languages when I was first teaching because I heard them so many times while my students shared answers on tests.

How do I know my students cheat on tests and quizzes? If I notice the very same wrong answers from two or more students who sat near each other during the test, I get suspicious. Then, my strategy is this: I make alternate forms for the next test. If it's multiple choice, I scramble the order of the choices. If it's true/false, I may either scramble the order or make a slight change to some of the items to change them from true to false or vice versa. For matching tests, I scramble one column. I try to be careful to make the alternate forms look quite similar, but may put a tiny A or B at the top of each. The results usually confirm my suspicions. When I return the quizzes and several students receive very low scores, I usually point out that they would have done better if they'd tried rather than looking for help from a neighbor. Then I have a chance to talk about how assessment drives my instruction and how important it is to be honest on tests so I can find out what they need help with.

> "I discuss what cheating means at the beginning of the semester, and during tests and quizzes I circulate around the room so that students know I'm watching."
>
> Leslie Sheen

My strategy may cause me a little additional work, but here's a secret. I usually create alternate forms just once to make a point. Then in subsequent tests, I give everyone the *same* form, but I take a pen and put the letter *A* on the top of half of the papers and *B* on the top of the other half, and very carefully distribute them A-B-A-B, making a pretty big show of this. The students generally believe that there are two forms, but I only have to make one key.

Now, of course, some teachers avoid the potential of cheating by giving tests that are more open-ended. For example, Celia Leckey writes, "I give tests and quizzes where students must write short answers or paragraphs rather than do multiple choice exercises. It minimizes cheating and is better for their linguistic development." I agree about the value of such tests, but I also believe that to test reading comprehension or other skills that I expect to be automatic, like vocabulary, then matching, T/F, very short answer, or multiple choice tests are valuable. I also want students to get used to formats like multiple choice, as they may not be familiar with them and will most likely be taking such tests in some of their content courses. And finally, I don't want to create too much extra work for myself. Easy-to-grade quizzes have a place in my classes, but easy-to-grade often means easy-to-cheat-on.

> **Megan Calvert is looking** for a solution to the problem of cheating in her classes: "Putting piles of books in between my students did nothing in my last class, nor did explaining the negative consequences of cheating."

Student-to-student communication during tests is not the only way to cheat, but it has been the most prevalent form of cheating in my classes. I often sit at the teacher's desk during tests. Recently, when a student came to the desk to ask a question about the test, I instinctively leaned to the side to look around her at the class. I wondered what that was about, until I realized that I've been conditioned to expect that once the question-asker shields me, two or more other students are sure to start talking. That's when I started a new policy: Call me over if you have a question or are finished, and don't stand in front of me!

If I need to get some grading done while students are taking a test (as I often want to return some homework in the same class), I have started sitting in the back of the room to do that work. Elizabeth Rasmussen also does this. She writes, "If I want to do some planning or grading while they're taking a test, I sit at a desk in the back. They can't tell where I'm looking or when I might get up."

I've had a few other cheating incidents recently. First, there's the old writing-on-the-desk trick. A couple of years ago, my colleagues and I decided that having students read a story, turn in the paper, and re-write the story from memory would be a good way to test what we'd been teaching—past verbs, articles, punctuation, etc. It has been a pretty good test, except when students cheat. The first or second time we used this test type, as I was straightening up the chairs after my students left the room I noticed sentences from the story written on the desks! Why hadn't we anticipated this? Since then, when I give that task, I tell the students that it's normal to want to take notes on the story—but our purpose is to have the story go through the filter of their memory and come out in their voice. And for that reason, instead of bringing the paper with the story printed on it to me, I will be coming by to pick it up, check their desk, and give them a clean sheet of paper to write on.

> **Karen Van Horn tries** to be proactive and to use a little humor: "At the beginning of the semester, I show them what cheating LOOKS like, and I act it out—hiding my eyes, stretching and leaning, dropping a pencil. Then I demonstrate acceptable thinking behavior—looking at the ceiling, furrowing my brow. Or if they must look at someone, I encourage them to look at me."

In another incident, a student brought in a pre-written essay. I thought I was being reasonable, and I told the class the day before the test, "We have been reading and writing about friendship a lot, so our in-class essay topic will be something about friends or friendship." One student turned in a very nice essay that was *not* on the topic of the test, but *was* about friends. I believe she wrote it at home and simply brought it into the room. Since then, I often supply the paper for important essays. I run a highlighter over the edge of the stack of sheets so that there is a faint bit of color on each sheet. I tell the students that since I'll be reading so many papers, I'd like them all to be the same size sheets. I don't think it's necessary to say, "I don't trust you," but the exam proctor's motto should be "trust but verify."

I got this idea from one of my undergraduate classes, in Madrid, Spain, of all places. In one of my classes, the professor gave us the topic of the final essay ahead of time. She told us we could prepare as much as we wanted at home, we could even write the entire essay, but that we must show up for the test with just a pen. She would provide the paper and we would write (or re-write from memory) the essay in class. I recall that the university had paper with the name of the division at the top: "Facultad de Filosofía y Letras." One of my classmates took home some sheets of that paper, wrote out his essay, smuggled it into the class and turned that in. The problem (for him) was, our professor brought in paper that day from the "Facultad de Filología." Obviously, the cheater was caught—and this future teacher got a great idea!

Finally, stories about using cell phones to cheat are probably very common these days. We have seen it all in my program. In a couple of cases we suspect that the topic was texted or emailed to someone (a native speaker) who quickly wrote compositions and sent them back to the cheaters, who then copied them onto their papers. We suspect this because the essays were all written in the same style and voice and did not at all match what the students had written under other circumstances. We give our students one to two hours for a composition that is only about 300 words, so it's not inconceivable that a native speaker could dash something off pretty quickly and email it, and the cheater could copy it and turn it in within the time limit.

More typically, students access the Internet on their phones during essay tests. We try to give accessible topics to our intermediate students—topics such as "write advice to a friend on how to be a good roommate." The problem is, the Internet is full of advice on being a good roommate. Of course it doesn't take long to detect this kind of cheating. Just put a string of words inside quotation marks into a search engine, and the website will pop up. But it's very sad when a student fails the class because he tried this on the final writing. Every semester I tell my class how easy this is for me to detect. I insist that cell phones be put away for the test, and allow only paper dictionaries. I walk around some, but as Nigel Caplan writes, "I'm not going to play the honesty police!"

> **Brian Anthon keeps** an eye on his students during tests and in-class essays. He advises, "Separate the desks as much as possible, walk around, and actively observe each student. If someone is constantly staring at their lap, they have either (a) just discovered that they have a lap or (b) are cheating."

Teachers may suggest having students leave their cell phones on the teacher's desk, but I'm not comfortable with this. How am I to know who is picking up whose phone at the end of the test? And besides, I have old cell phones hanging around my house. If I wanted to cheat, I'd simply put some old phone on the teacher's desk and sit in the back of the room with my real phone. So I don't think collecting students' phones is the answer.

Another strategy many teachers employ to teach an important lesson about how cheating is viewed in our culture, as Vivian Leskes notes, is to "give both the transmitter and receiver of information a zero." This usually shocks the transmitter in my class, as I apply this rule not only on tests but also on homework assignments. My sense from talking with my students over the years is that American classrooms are much more competitive than classrooms in cultures that value cooperation over competition. If a teacher is grading "on a curve," it doesn't really matter how well a student does on the test as long as he or she does better than the rest of the class. This is incentive, in our culture that values GPA so highly, for students not to share answers.

My stronger students need to know about this American classroom culture and sometimes need to be instructed—and persuaded—not to share their work. Once I make this clear, I offer some tips. I show people strategies I used in high school to hide my test paper from the eyes of my neighbors. Do not pick your paper up; if it's flat on the desk it is harder for your neighbor to see. Use your arm or hand or eraser or pencil box to cover your responses. And I tell students what to say when a classmate asks to copy their homework. I tell them to lie if necessary. If you don't feel that you can flat out refuse to cheat, I tell them, "Say you didn't do the homework. Say you left it in your car. Say you are ashamed to show it since you are sure you did it all wrong."

Finally, sometimes we brainstorm and write compositions on the topic of cheating. One fun topic is about very creative ways students cheat—we brainstorm together and students write about the most outrageous cheating techniques they can think of. I do this more to say, "I know all of the tricks so don't try any" than to give them ideas. They usually come up with ideas like writing on body parts, leaving a book in the restroom and asking for a break during the test, writing on the inside of the label of a water bottle, and more! I store all of these ideas in my memory bank.

13 Chatting, Helping Cheating?

In classes where we begin collaboration on day one, it's sometimes hard to stop that collaboration when it needs to stop. Teachers craft routines and procedures to communicate to students when it's appropriate to chat or help a neighbor and when it's time to quiet down. And our ESL classes are often the first time our students experience the very American concept of "do your own work" that is drilled into us from kindergarten. Failing a quiz or homework assignment, even when the offender is the transmitter and not the receiver of the information, is an uncomfortable experience but also a valuable step toward becoming successful in an American education system.

Chapter 14
Smart Phones: Friend or Foe?

As has been mentioned a few times, this book is a snapshot in time. This latest snapshot deals with smart phones and tablets. A few years ago, the biggest intrusion cell technology made in my class was the occasional ring, or a ping from a dying battery. Now, at my college at least, a student who does not have a smart phone is in the minority. Teachers need to deal with this explosion of technology. Some embrace it, some accommodate it, and some regulate it. This chapter deals with several issues related to our students'—and our—smart phones.

Ringing Phones

Having cell phones ring in class seems to be a very popular example of a classroom management issue. We see reports on the internet or videos on social media. We hear anecdotes about professors who answer students' phones when they ring or insist that students answer them on speaker phone. But is this a big issue in our classes? In fact, only 10 percent of respondents noted that having cell phones ring in class is a common disruption (see Figure 20). While it may happen occasionally—and I confess that mine has rung at least once!—as Nina Liakos notes, "Smart phones are just part of the student 'body' now," so an occasional intrusive ring is not unexpected. Indeed, as more people give up land lines and use their cell phones exclusively, we are sure to note more ringing phones in our classes.

Nina Liakos continues, "Sometimes I ask students to turn off their phones, but this also turns off their dictionaries these days! So I ask them to silence the phones. I used to confiscate the phones for the class, but I've given that up."

I generally try to make a show of silencing my phone as I get my class materials ready. I feel that this shows that I'm a regular person who has a phone just like them and likes to be available to family and friends, but that the two hours I'm in class are *time away from my phone*. Claire

Cirolia has the same strategy: "At the start of the term, and the start of each class, I show the students that I turn off my phone and put it away, and require them to do the same."

> Donna Tortorella explains that, if a phone rings in her class, "I usually put my hand to my ear (pretending it's a phone) and say, 'Please tell your girlfriend/boyfriend 11:00—that's when class is over.'"

In the rules-are-made-to-be-broken (or at least amended) column, I'd like to add that on occasion I allow phones to ring. A recent example comes to mind: A student's wife was expecting a baby any day, and he told me that she might be calling him. I allowed him to keep his phone on and simply asked that he leave the room as soon as a call came in. Sometimes I use that example in my talk about cell phone rules, making the point that this is a very, very rare occurrence and that their "emergency" had better be a real one. I've also had parents slip out to answer a call from their children's school, but in these cases the phones seem to be on vibrate, as I don't notice the ring. If this happens more than once, however, I have a talk with the student as it seems that "a call from the school" could be a cover for just about anything. If it is indeed the school calling frequently, the student may need some help navigating the system. In other words, this may be bigger than a simple class disruption.

> Elisabeth Chan deals with a ringing phone this way: "I ask the student to put the phone away. After a warning, I may ask them to leave and 'take care of their emergency.'"

Texting and the Internet

More annoying for me is when students use their phones to text or access the Internet. Nearly 30 percent of teachers surveyed share my annoyance (see Figure 20).

Jane Stanga writes, "I remind students to have their phones stored in a purse or bag during class. Occasionally, a student is texting under their desk during class. If it's the first time, I usually just remind them to put the phone away. If the student continues the behavior, I have taken the phone and placed it on my desk for the duration of the class."

I had a major problem with a young man and his phone in a recent semester. I find it hard to require that phones be completely put away unless we are having a test, since for many students their phone is also their clock and their dictionary. In fact, this student always claimed that he was looking up a word when I asked him to put the phone down. So I started "encouraging" him not to look up every unfamiliar word. I finally had to pull him out of the class and ban the use of the phone. Not surprisingly, he did not pass the class. Whatever "strategy" he was using, whether it was indeed looking up a word every couple of minutes, playing a game, or chatting via text message with someone, it was not a successful one. I never took the phone from him, however, as I am not comfortable having something so valuable in my possession—even if it's just sitting on the desk in the classroom.

Perhaps the reason it bothers us less when a phone rings is because this is most likely an oversight—the student forgot to silence the phone. But texting or updating a Facebook status requires a conscious effort to "leave" the class.

Smart Phones as Tools

The reason that phones are out at all on my students' desks is because they are useful tools in an interactive, student-centered classroom. For example, my students don't carry a bulky learner's dictionary but instead use an app on their phone or access a good dictionary on the Internet. When they are working in groups, if they need to look something up on the Internet, on Blackboard, or on our college website, often at least one student in the group will have a smart phone for this. If they need to time themselves giving a presentation or reading something, the phone can be a timer. If they want to record themselves speaking or reading, they can do that—often asking a groupmate to hold the phone while they talk or read. If they want to practice with a PowerPoint, they can often pull that up on a tablet. Smart phones have made my class a better place, so I tend to put up with the occasional ring or text message. Not everyone agrees with me, however, and I certainly see their perspective. For example, Karen Vlaskamp notes, "In general, students shouldn't have their devices out unless it's 'dictionary time.' While there are valid educational uses, our current students are too distracted by their devices. They need 100 percent focus on class." I think we need to find our comfort zone—perhaps class by class, and for me this may depend on the maturity level of my class as well as the skill area we are working on.

> "Technology is here to stay. Might as well integrate it into the class."
>
> Virginia Cabasa-Hess

One area we should explore is in using apps to help our students learn. Good learner dictionary apps are quite expensive, but students may want to consider them. There are also more low-cost apps for pronunciation, and many free apps. One that I recommended to my spelling class is Boggle. I found it a great way to reinforce common spelling patterns.

Recently my college moved from paper course evaluations to an online system. Several teachers were worried that our normal 100 percent completion rate for course evaluations would plummet. Then they realized that students could access the evaluations during class time, using the college wi-fi on their phones. The few students who didn't have a smart phone used the class computer. Once the teachers got the class started, they were able to leave the room just as they did in the days of paper evaluation forms.

Using smart phones or tablets while working in groups or to access apps or online course materials during class is one thing, and using them to record, film, or photograph the teacher or the classroom is another. When asked about recording explanations, 70 percent of teachers responded that they don't mind if students ask to do this, but most replied that students haven't asked (see Figure 21). Chris Feak points out, "Anything that helps students learn is fine with me." I agree, as long as everyone has equal opportunity in the class.

I teach a spelling class in which I work hard to have students hear the vowel sounds of English. I encourage students to record parts of

Figure 21

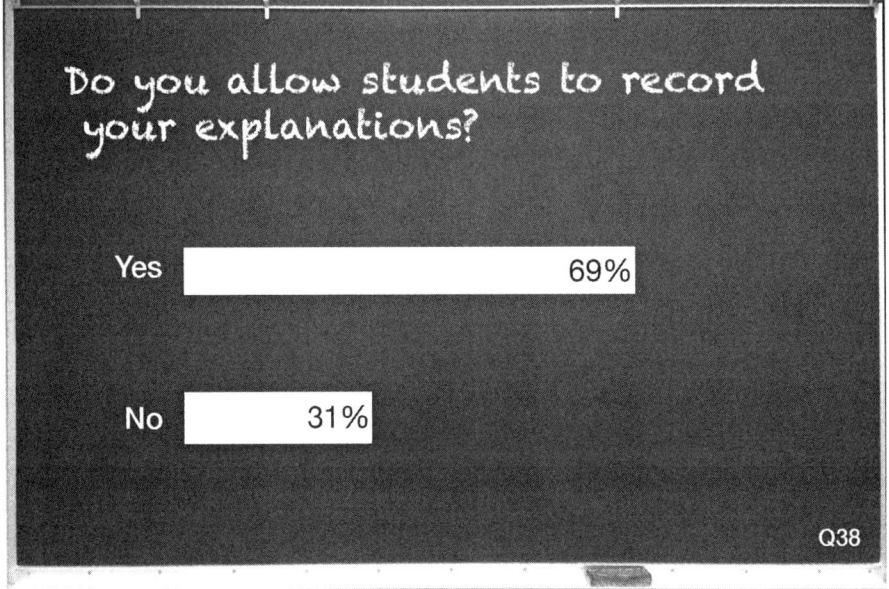

the class—and I even note this on the course syllabus—but students rarely do. I often record myself, however, and post the recording on Blackboard.

DeAnna Coon writes, "I think audio recordings are helpful to auditory learners; maybe they just need to hear it again, and why would I frown upon that?" And Tom Hilanto notes, "The ability to review notes and discussion from the class outside of class will reinforce their overall progress."

Recently, I've had a couple of students pull out their phones and tablets and start to record me without asking first, and certainly without prompting by me. I wasn't completely comfortable with it for a couple of reasons. In the first instance, I was giving my quick review of the format of several rhetorical patterns on the day before the final exam. I empathized with the student who wanted to capture that on her tablet, but it was very distracting for everyone in the room to have her (quite large) tablet held aloft! I said, "I really don't think you need to record this," and she stopped. In the second instance, I was giving a sample presentation in my academic oral skills class. I noticed a few phones aimed at me and realized I was about to be recorded. This was a problem for me. If two or three people had a recording of my voice and my

PowerPoint slides, that would give them an unfair advantage as they prepared their speeches. After that I had someone record me with *my* tablet, and I uploaded the file to my private YouTube channel and gave everyone in the class access. I find I'm doing that more and more to reduce the temptation for everyone to pull out a phone once one student sets the precedent. As Janice Hornyak notes, "I'd find a bunch of students watching me explain through their cell phones as they recorded to be awkward and distancing, but so far I haven't had anyone want to do that."

> "I appreciate it if they ask when they're recording the class. It always takes me time to get used to that."
>
> *Wendy Asplin*

Privacy is certainly a concern with today's recording capabilities. In fact, Elisabeth Chan prohibits recording in her class because she is concerned about privacy. She writes, "I don't want students to record explanations—either audio or video—because I feel that it gets into the question of property. I don't want my lectures posted online for the public to hear/see." Perhaps as more teachers and entire programs move to deliberately flip their classrooms, these ad hoc recording opportunities will be replaced with pre-recorded clips that we can post for students to view and share freely.

> "I encourage the use of technology when appropriate, but no texting in class!"
>
> *Kathleen Wax*

Teachers are more likely to allow students to take photographs, usually with their smart phones. In fact, 87 percent of teachers surveyed reported that they allow students to photograph notes or PowerPoint slides, but many don't encourage the practice (see Figure 22).

On one end of a continuum are teachers like Rebecca Wolff, who writes, "Taking a picture of the board drives me crazy, and I will actually block the board or erase it quickly so that it can't be done. I think that

Figure 22

students are not learning how to take notes, and they have no idea how valuable the action of writing something down is. I do a lot of lessons on note-taking, and I expect my students to do it."

On the other end of the continuum are teachers like DeAnna Coon, who reports, "It's more time efficient for both me and the students if they want to take pictures of my notes; they can also come back and indicate anything they had questions about without it being an awkward exchange trying to make me remember and understand what they're referring back to." And Cathy Dutchak notes, "Since mine are speaking and listening classes with a note-taking component, I allow them to photograph the class-compiled notes, to compare them with theirs." This to me seems like a very good use of the camera on a smart phone; something that would, without the smart-phone camera, be impossible to do.

Many years ago I heard a talk about integrating technology into instruction. The speaker warned us, "Do not use the vacuum to beat the carpets." I took that advice to heart. Technology shouldn't be used to do things that are best accomplished without technology. In this case, photographing the blackboard is not a substitute for learning how to take notes. But when it's more expeditious to snap a photo, why not? As long as everyone has equal access to the photos and no one has an unfair advantage in the class, I think we should allow it.

> "**The more integrated** technology becomes on our lives, the more I believe we will have to integrate it into the classroom. If it's more efficient to take a photo, I think it's a smart choice. The real world would applaud efficiency."
>
> *Megan Calvert*

Of course there are caveats. Again, students can't use their smart-phone cameras to avoid learning how to take notes in their second language. As Stephanie Sareeram writes, "I allow photos of notes on the board, though they must listen to my spiel each time of how writing things by hand enhances neural pathways to form. I find that weaker students are the photographers and stronger students hear my warning." And Lori Ward points out, "I don't mind if they take a picture of notes on the chalkboard, but I would not want them to take a picture of an answer key that I put on the document camera, for example." This is why it's best to limit the photography to the last few minutes of the class. Janice Hornyak writes, "If they want to photograph the board at the END of class, that's okay, but electronics are supposed to be put away when I'm explaining something."

And of course, smart-phone photographers can be teachers as well. Marilyn Odaka writes, "I've also taken photos with my iPhone of student-generated work on the board and posted it on Blackboard so students can later use it for review or reference." And many teachers report posting their PowerPoint slides for students to view at home as well—much more efficient than having students photograph each slide.

As students and teachers alike use phones and tablets more as tools in our classes—to access what is posted for students online, to use functions such as the timer, the recorder, the camera, dictionary or pronunciation apps—we have to put up with or otherwise regulate annoyances like rings and having students text or use social media in class. In all, I believe it's safe to say that smart phones and tablets are here to stay and the changes they are having on our classrooms are permanent.

Classroom Trouble Spots: Wrap-Up

I recently had a negative experience that snuck up on me. I taught a very intensive summer class—five hours per day, four days a week for eight weeks, and all of the 24 students were new to my program except for two very weak ones who were repeating the class. I tried to create community and class rules in the first week while accommodating some late arrivals and moving out a student whose level was too high, but we were really moving very quickly through the material. As I mentioned earlier, by about the third class I am beyond the whole "creating community/establishing rules" thing and into teaching.

Somewhere in the second half of the session, I realized that I had several problems. I was bothered by unauthorized breaks, students returning very late from our scheduled breaks, extensive chatting in the back of the room, and excessive cell phone use. Luckily there was no cheating, but I was exhausted from trying to deal with these behaviors while keeping the learning going. Then, one day it hit me that many of the students were addressing me as "Teacher." "Teacher, what pages did we have for homework?" "Teacher, can you help us with this exercise?" "Teacher, I can't think of a good conclusion for my composition." I think I had been so focused on downplaying the negative behaviors and focusing on the learning that I didn't notice at first. By the time I noticed, I really felt like it was too late to address the "Teacher" issue. Upon reflection I realized who the source was—one vocal student who actually missed the first two days of class. I should have pulled her aside and told her that she should call me by my name or "Professor." But once the teachable moment passed, I decided to choose other battles and let the "Teacher" title ride. Fast forward one year: That student showed up in my upper-level composition class. She had broken herself of this and any other negative behaviors and became a model student! Success.

The experience in my summer course reinforced for me that it is best to be aware of negative behaviors and address them early. One good alternative to harping on what the students are doing wrong is to praise positive behaviors—something I think I forget to do. When everyone is present at 8:00 on a rainy Friday, I'm sure they'd like to hear, "It's wonderful that you are all here and ready to learn. Thank you for that." When students quickly move into groups and get to work, you might say, "I'm so impressed at how fast you did that." When two or three students go to the board to get started on an exercise, it's nice to say, "Thank you, Carlos and Linh, for being brave enough to go first!" Successful student-centered classes have to start with the positive, but as my experience shows, we sometimes have to address the negative as well.

Making Connections

Challenging Beliefs: What Teachers Think

What's your opinion? Circle the extent to which you agree or disagree with this statement. To read survey responses to the statement, please turn to Appendix 1 (pages 183–185).

> Classes sometimes "click" and sometimes don't, in spite of what I do as the teacher.
>
> strongly agree   agree   neither agree nor disagree   disagree   strongly disagree

Classroom Connections: What Teachers Do

In a class you are teaching or visiting, you may want to consider some of these points about how trouble spots are handled.

1. During the first few weeks of the course, how are late additions to the class accommodated?
2. How is tardiness handled?
3. Do students take unscheduled breaks? If so, is this problematic?
4. Do students chat with neighbors? If so, is this problematic?
5. Are the concepts of helping vs. cheating or using sources vs. plagiarizing discussed?
6. If there is a quiz or test, what procedures are used to discourage cheating?
7. Do students have cell phones on their desks?
8. Are smart phones or tablets used as tools in the class?

Strategies and Motivations: What Teachers Say

Consider these comments from survey respondents on a few of the topics from this unit.

On planning for students who enter late:

Many programs allow students to enter classes on the second or third class meeting, and some students come into our classes after diagnostic testing and subsequent level change. Teachers often plan for this "revolving door."

    Donna Tortorella: "At the beginning of the semester, I give students folders for handouts, homework assignments, etc. I keep three extra folders and add each handout that I use in the first few classes. When a new student comes to class, we welcome him and I give him a folder at the end of his first class and explain what we've covered so far."

    Christina Luckey: "Use this as an opportunity to review names! It takes students so long to remember each other's names. Also, go over what we've done in class as a quick review (elicited from students). It helps me to see how much they've absorbed."

On dealing with tardy students:

Teachers seem to find ways to communicate expectations about on-time arrival by maintaining a focus on learning and by rewarding positive behaviors while perhaps ignoring negative ones.

    Elizabeth Whisnant: "If tardiness is a pattern, I will email the students and let them know they are missing out on important information. I avoid embarrassing or harassing students when they are late because I believe it's extremely important to have a welcoming classroom environment."

    Breana Bayraktar: "I haven't done any public shaming or making students wait in the hall to come in, but I have been known to remind a student who has come in late and then is asking questions about something we did before she arrived that 'we discussed X before you arrived; you need to get notes from someone about the material you missed.'"

Darlene Branges: "I tell students, 'Come in quickly and get with the class. If the door is closed, wait until it is open.' The door is closed during presentations."

On preventing cheating on quizzes and tests:

In a collaborative environment where we ask students over and over to help each other, we change our tune on test days and it becomes every student for himself. That is when we may turn from cheerleader to enforcer. Teachers weigh in on their thinking about strategies to limit cheating:

Karen Vlaskamp: "Nothing can be on their desk or table. If possible, I spread students out. When I feel I can't trust a class, I make two versions of the test; the questions are the same but maybe in a different order. Also, since most people have two hands on the desk when writing (one with the pencil, one holding the paper), I pay special attention to students with only one hand visible and those who seem to be 'meditating' (looking toward their laps)."

Stephanie Sareeram: "I minimize cheating two ways: with time and/or forms. With a narrow time limit, students don't have time to look around. With alternate forms, students who are geographically too close can't get much from their neighbor. All of that, plus I make full-class tests that have so many parts they can't cheat too easily because their neighbors rarely work at their speed or are too busy worrying that they'll finish."

Lisa Stelle: "I assign students different seats on test days, and the seats change for each test, so the students never know where they'll be sitting or who they will be sitting next to. Also, I have different sets of tests for each semester, so I rotate the tests from semester to semester. That way, if the student has a copy of the test from the previous semester, it won't help him/her since I'll give a different version this semester."

Judy Snyder: "I change tests regularly and make alternate editions of tests that are easy to cheat on (T/F, multiple choice, etc.). I almost always have a good amount of writing on my tests, so it's easy to see if someone has copied answers. If necessary, I limit bathroom breaks during tests."

On allowing students to record our classes:

Technology changes our teaching, and thus classroom rules sometimes need to change. Teachers need to consider how smart phones and tablets may be allowed or prohibited as recording devices in the classroom.

    Mike J. Waguespack: "I would rather not have students record my class. I want students to learn the kinds of language skills that they will need in other classes and in their future careers. If we don't push students to process the English that they encounter the first time, I don't believe they will develop the level of 'automaticity' that they will need."

    Jane Stanga: "I would prefer to have students improve their note-taking and listening skills rather than just photographing or recording notes and explanations."

    Judy Snyder: "I explain to students that they should always get the teacher's permission before recording anything. I also tell them that it is likely teachers will self-monitor, even if subconsciously, when they know they are being recorded. That's not necessarily bad, but it does create a different class atmosphere."

    Robyn Brinks Lockwood: "I'm still thinking through allowing my students to photograph or record my classes and how best to manage that. I don't really have a problem with photographs except that I must make sure the phones don't stay out and Facebook is not being checked. I do ask students NOT to post photographs or recordings; I ask that they be for personal use only."

    Antonina Rodgers: "I have used my iPhone and iPad as a student. I try to treat my students as adults and allow the use of technology as long as it's not disruptive and doesn't lead to academic dishonesty."

Appendix 1: Challenging Beliefs

At the end of each unit, you considered a statement related to the topic of that unit. This section presents survey respondents' reactions to and comments about those statements.

Unit One

See Figure 23. When I was a young teacher, I may have indicated "agree" because, being the same age as or even younger than my students meant that I may have had trouble acting like an authority figure. Today I might check "agree" for the opposite reason. I might be older than my students' parents, but I don't want to seem out of tune with popular culture or to be unapproachable. I want them to see me as a collaborator in the learning process, yet I need to maintain some authority.

Some comments from survey respondents, at least two-thirds of whom disagree with this statement (see Figure 23) follow:

"I find this difficult with some groups of students, but not all. I think part of it is age related; I sometimes have students who are my age or even older. They may view me as a peer instead of an authority, or not old enough to be experienced and have something to teach them."—DeAnna Coon

"With younger students, I want them to look forward to coming to my class, to participate actively, take risks, be goofy at times. I am playful and energetic, but this can work against me sometimes. It can be hard to rein students in once they have 'let their hair down' a bit."—Suzanne Mele Szwarcewicz

"This really depends on the maturity level of the students. If they are more mature, I can be more friendly and not have to worry that they will misinterpret my role, take advantage, and stop following rules." —Kay Marshall

"I position myself in the role of 'guide' as opposed to 'judge' or 'parent.'"—W. Riley Holzberlein

Figure 23

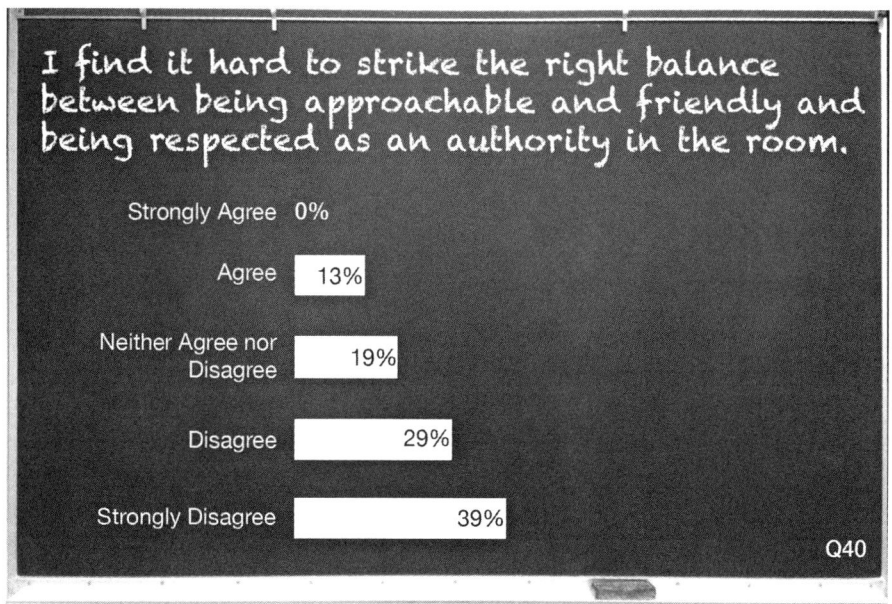

"I found this hard as a novice teacher. Now I'm comfortable with my authority, and I no longer see my job as being students' friend—I'm there to teach."—Nigel Caplan

"I strike a balance naturally. I don't know why. I really think it is something that is very difficult to learn from a book or training. It comes from personality and experience."—Allyson Noble

"I don't find this a problem, despite being on the young(ish) side. I am confident in my abilities as a teacher and as a modeler of the English language, and I believe that this confidence allows me to be approachable, but always respected. Plus, I believe that my sincere desire for my students to perform well is very clear to them, as is the fact that I hold very high expectations for them."—Breana Bayraktar

"Several years ago, I would have checked a different answer, but now I feel that I have found the right balance with my students. They all know that I am a strict teacher and that I enforce the classroom policies, but they would also say that I am nice and that I care about them. I think my experience and learning from my mistakes has helped me to find this balance. It took a while to figure everything out."—Lisa Stelle

"In general, I can find the right balance, but I still think it's difficult, particularly at the start of a new class, because each class has a different make-up of students. I try to adapt how strict I need to be based on that student make-up."—Marilyn Odaka

"Being approachable/friendly and respected as an authority are not mutually exclusive. In fact, I would argue that a friendly, caring teacher would receive greater respect from the students."—Tom Hilanto

Unit Two

See Figure 24. I've carried this thought with me for the better part of three decades. I can still vividly remember hearing Dr. Robert DiPietro say this in a talk at Georgetown University, where I was teaching in the IEP. Professor DiPietro—whom I'd had for several courses as an undergrad and whom I truly respected—was most likely promoting his teaching technique that he called "strategic interaction," in which the teacher creates scenarios within which language develops in the classroom. This was the 1980s, of course, and many of us were still using bits of the audio-lingual method. I, as a young teacher, was convinced at the time that I was in control of the learning. I bristled when he said this! I thought, "If I am teaching adjective clauses, they WILL LEARN adjective clauses!" Once my initial shock passed, I did see his point. Now, over and over I see that what we are actively engaged in in my class may not be truly internalized for many months. I may have goals and objectives, but I believe that what students take away, and when they master it, is really out of my control.

Some comments from survey respondents, who seem fairly evenly split on their opinion of this statement (see Figure 24) follow:

"I disagree with this insofar as I feel I AM responsible for the learning of the class as a whole. I cannot be in control of what any particular student learns, but if large numbers of my students are not learning, then I have to question what I am teaching and/or how I am teaching it."—Mike J. Waguespack

"We can never fully control another person, but we can provide opportunities for people to learn."—Kathleen Wax

"Perhaps 'control' is too strong of a word. I'm a firm believer that it's a two-way street in the classroom—I have responsibilities and so do all my students. They must take responsibility for their learning;

Figure 24

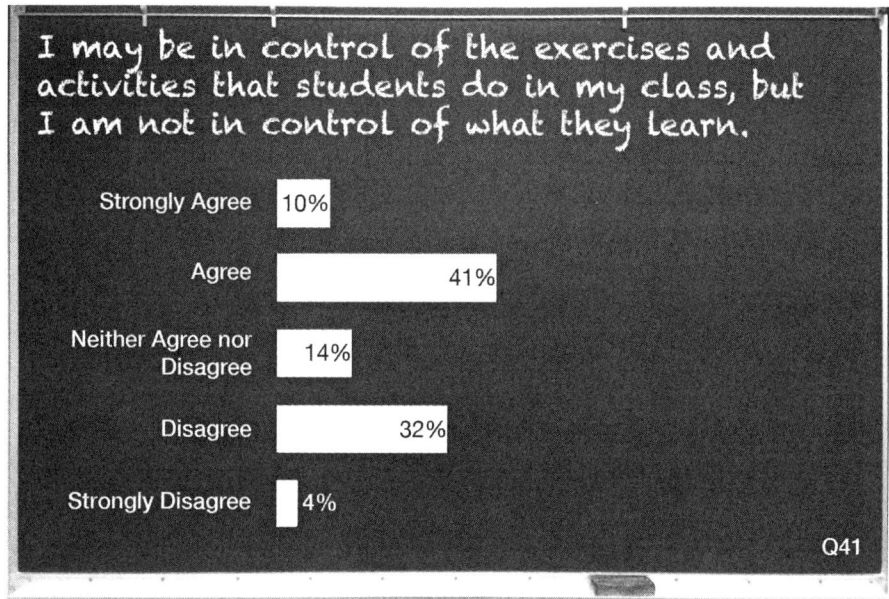

however, as the teacher, I can and should use my position to facilitate this learning."—Claire Cirolia

"This is an area I'm trying to work on and improve each semester—reminding myself (and my students) how much of the total learning is their responsibility."—Elizabeth Rasmussen

"Teachers provide support, but don't learn for students."—Darlene Branges

"While I strongly agree that students must have the desire to learn, the path to learning should be set by the instructor. Creating a safe learning environment where creativity and collaboration are combined with activities that lead to a specific learning outcome is a good step to influence the learning process."—Tom Hilanto

"I try to create a good learning environment, I present well-prepared lessons, and I give plenty of opportunity for practice. If students have difficulty or are not doing well, I offer assistance but do not force them to accept my assistance, as they are, in the end, responsible for their learning."—Bill Woodard

"I learned long ago not to take credit for student successes but also not to blame myself for student failures to learn."—Nina Liakos

Unit Three

See Figure 25. I was glad to see that three-quarters of the respondents agreed with this statement as sort of validation that I am not being too sensitive or critical of my students. I try to remind myself that sometimes I'm more enthusiastic about my classes than my students are. But that doesn't stop me from being irritated that my students work through exercises, edit papers, memorize words, and more, without ever seeing or even asking about the big picture. This is particularly bothersome to me when students are working in pairs or groups and they rush through an exercise without focusing on the learning goals that I have in mind.

This may, of course, be the fault of some of my assignments. Say, for example, I give students 20 sentences that need gerunds, with the base form of the verb supplied in parentheses. If I were the student, I'd fill in the forms slowly, while reading each sentence—preferably aloud. Then I'd probably memorize the sentences or at least the collocations. But how many of my students simple write the verbs on the blanks without even reading the sentences? Or worse, if they need to fill in infinitives, the student writes *to – to – to – to – to – to –* down the column, then goes back to fill in the verbs. Yes, that got the job done, but why don't they see that we're providing (mostly meaningful) examples? And yes, I tell them how I believe they should do these exercises. Write it, say it, memorize it, put it away, and review it later.

Similarly, students edit papers that I've marked with symbols without investing in understanding why they made the error that I marked. They memorize vocabulary in isolation without rereading the articles that the words came from, in spite of my begging and cajoling. I bite my tongue to avoid nagging or sounding exasperated!

Some comments from respondents, who seem less frustrated than I feel (see Figure 27) follow:

"I have to remind myself daily that while language is my passion, for most of my students it's just a required course."—George A. Flowers

"Yes, this happens when students are tired from working the night shift or staying up with their sick child. Sometimes they have their minds on other things. It's human nature, I think."—Claire Cirolia

Figure 25

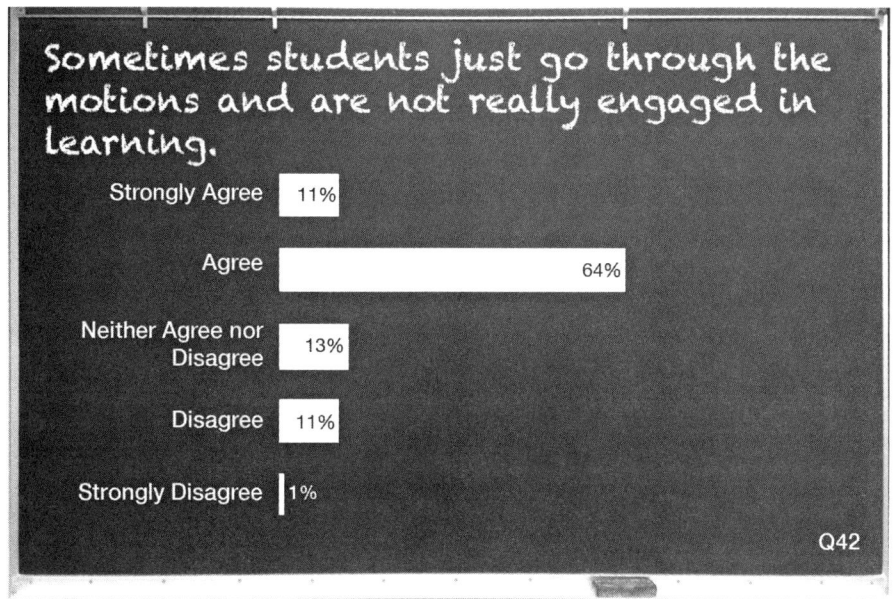

"In any class anywhere, if a student does not feel he/she really needs to fully acquire the skills, then going through the motions is the typical result. An instructor can only hope to change their minds." —Brian Anthon

"One of my greatest challenges is to help students learn how to help themselves to learn, but overall, I feel that most of my students ARE actively engaged in learning at some level."—Mike J. Waguespack

"Unfortunately, this does happen with a few students, so I ask myself to what extent should I be changing something in the class to engage them more, or are they just unmotivated to respond to anything in the classroom?"—Kay Marshall

Unit Four

See Figure 26. I was happy to see that most respondents chose agree or strongly agree on this item. I enjoy bringing humor into many of my classes—self-deprecating stories of my life, short anecdotes and jokes, or funny stories to read. I still remember the few (very few) jokes I learned

Figure 26

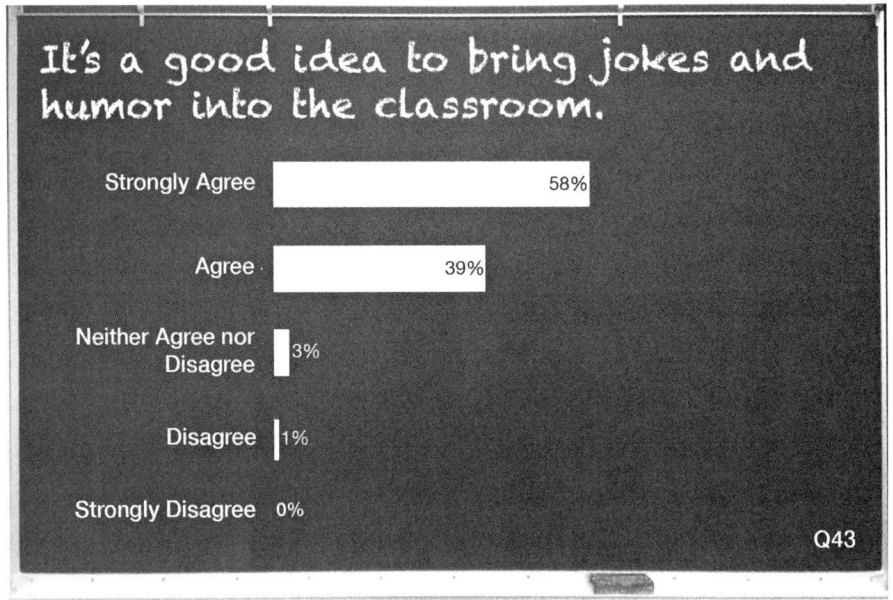

in Spanish and repeat them whenever I get an audience. I think I was so proud that I understood and remembered them, and I find the same reaction from my students.

I once had a colleague who used to say she was flattered when students chose to follow her to a higher level, but the downside was that they already knew all of her jokes. I agree! I use humorous anecdotes to teach grammar points, from verbs to articles to punctuation. I often use jokes that I remember from my childhood. I use silly tension-breaking jokes like pretending to forget to bring their test to class or forgetting to assign homework. In my composition class, sometimes we brainstorm and write about "how to be an annoying classmate," coming up with silly examples like bringing stinky food to class and getting crumbs on everyone's papers. People who are just learning how to navigate in a second language love to join in, and it's so encouraging to see their voice develop when they try to inject humor into their writing. I've even played April Fool's jokes on some classes, but never anything mean. I do understand that one has to gauge the comfort level of the class before joking around, but my funny anecdotes are a part of every class.

Some comments from respondents, who have plenty of caveats when it comes to using humor (see Figure 26) follow:

"I enjoy a good laugh as long as the humor is appropriate for the language level of the students and is not done at anyone's expense." —Jane Stanga

"Usually the humor is self-deprecating. When using humor, you have to know your students and how they will react."—Karen Vlaskamp

"Laughter is energizing. My class goes for four and a half hours. If we don't laugh, it's dreadful."—Karen Van Horn

"Laughter lowers the affective filter."—Nina Liakos

"Humor helps students feel comfortable, and it's hard for them to learn if they're not at ease and feel they can be open with me. Even though I want to maintain high standards, there's no reason why we can't all smile and laugh frequently in class."—Judy Snyder

"I sometimes use humor directed at myself (though not at the beginning of the semester). You have to know your class. I think gentle humor and laughter can add to learning." —Mary Charleza

"I usually tell some embarrassing stories of my travels abroad, and that makes the class lighter."—Samantha Parkes

"Humor really helps to establish a social presence with the students and aids in creating a comfort factor between students and faculty." —Til Turner

"Life is short and very hard. People need to laugh."—Dana Kappler

Unit Five

See Figure 27. I think I tend to take a lot of responsibility for whether my classes 'click' or not—perhaps too much given that two-thirds of respondents feel that this statement is true. I feel very, very good when I have a great group, and I'll confess to thinking that I had something to do with that. And when the groups don't click, I go over and over in my mind what I perhaps did wrong. Deep down, of course, I'm sure I'm not responsible, and I am grateful to those students who make the group great and to those who stick it out in a group that doesn't quite mesh.

Some comments from respondents, who report that most classes do indeed "click" (see Figure 27) follow:

"I think I can certainly help students form a cohesive group and set up an appropriate atmosphere in the room, but some classes are more

Figure 27

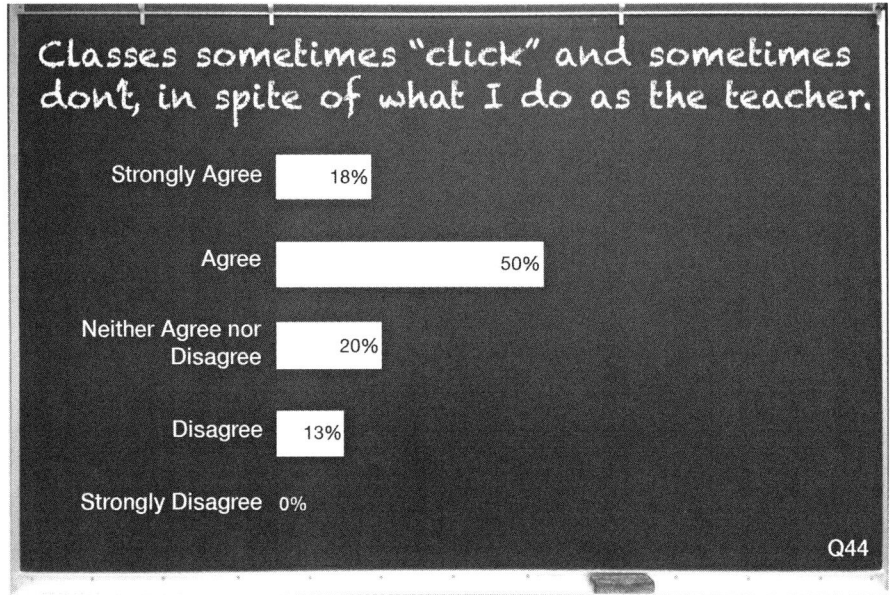

challenging than others. In general, though, group work helps increase the chances that the classes will 'click.'"—Nataliya Schetchikova

"Most of the time, my classes 'click,' but on occasion they don't. All it takes is one 'angry at life' person to change the dynamics of the class. When this happens, I just continue being a professional with goals but work harder to reach them with humor."—Dana Kappler

"If I feel that a class doesn't 'click,' I always begin by asking myself, 'What can I do better?' I try many things, and if it still doesn't 'click,' then I decide to keep trying my best, no matter how they respond."—Leslie Sheen

"I can set a friendly tone and make sure they treat each other with respect, but some classes click better than others."—Laurie Barton

"For the most part, classes begin to gel over the course of the semester, and surprising friendships are formed by the group work. However, I have had a single negative person make it difficult for everyone and prevent the class from clicking."—Elizabeth Whisnant

"Sometimes you can just get a difficult mix. I once had a class where 80 percent of students were from one language group, one country, and one program sponsored by their government! It was impossible to stop them from speaking their first language in small groups, and the other students complained. Despite all my efforts, I was counting the days until the semester ended!"—Elizabeth Rasmussen

"This semester, I had a challenging group of students. They were very quiet, and my usual 'tricks' didn't work. It did get better, but I couldn't do some of the activities that I usually do."—Karen Vlaskamp

"You can't force students to like or enjoy one another. You can try community-building activities and exercises, but a lot of it comes down to personalities and interests, so while the community might improve due to my efforts, it may never be completely cohesive."—DeAnna Coon

"Fortunately, this is rare, but I have vivid memories of groups that just didn't gel—clashes of personalities, clashes of values, differences in the importance given to being in college. I have no remedy for this. Thankfully, college teachers can always look forward to the next semester and a new group of students!"—Judy Snyder

"I once taught a class where every one of the 23 students was from a different country, and from different age groups. It was one of the most dynamic classes I've had the privilege of teaching. Students came early and stayed later, and the discussion offered a remarkable variety of viewpoints."—Tom Hilanto

"Every class has a personality. Some you wish you could bottle and save . . . others make you glad semesters have ends."—Janice Hornyak

Appendix 2: The Survey

This Appendix presents the original survey that respondents completed. Survey question numbers are indicated at the bottom of the figures throughout the book to enable you to see each original question in the context of the entire survey. Additional responses to some items appear in Appendix 3 as well.

Student-Centered Learning in the ESL Classroom

Thank you for taking time to complete this survey. I will use your input as I write a book on ESL classroom management, to be published in 2015. To thank you for your time, I'd like to send you a copy of the book once it is published. It is tentatively titled *Managing the ESL Classroom.*

    This project is supported with a President's Sabbatical from Northern Virginia Community College. I am grateful for the time and support the college is offering.

    I look forward to reading your ideas and opinions. Thank you again for your time.

Janet Giannotti

PART ONE: Setting the Tone in Your Classroom

1. How important is it for you to set the tone in your <u>first</u> class meeting?

___ very important
___ I usually use the first week or so to set the tone.
___ not so important; I like to let class personalities emerge.

2. Do you use an icebreaker on the first day of class? If you would like to share your favorite ice breaker, please type in the box below.

3. Do you have any tips on how to learn students' names quickly?

4. Many teachers believe classes run smoothly if everyone knows the rules. What are the two or three most important rules in your classroom?

5. How do you communicate class rules to students? Please check the statement that most closely matches your approach.

___ I provide students with a syllabus on the first day that outlines my class rules and policies.
___ I provide a syllabus with some basic information, and then students brainstorm rules.
___ I institute rules as the class progresses and I learn more about their habits and personalities.
___ I don't have any rules in my class.
___ Other (Please explain)

188 Appendix 2

6. What is your stand on the use of students' L1 in your classroom?
___ I have an "English-only" policy.
___ I allow students to use their L1 to chat quietly, especially about instructions.
___ I encourage students to explain concepts and instructions to each other in their L1.

Comments:

7. In many programs, students are often permitted to join the class late – a few days or a week into the term. Do you have any tips on welcoming and/or integrating a student who joins late?

8. What is your stand on bringing controversial topics into the classroom?
___ I generally steer students away from controversial topics.
___ I deal with topics if they come up.
___ I like to use controversial topics in my classes.
Comment?

9. In a student-centered classroom, students should feel free to ask questions. This, however, can be problematic. Which of the following do you see as inappropriate or disturbing to the flow of your class? Please check all that apply.
____ One student asks too many questions.
____ If the class is working on grammar exercises, a student asks about the meaning of a word.
____ If I'm explaining a grammar point (e.g., present perfect), a student asks about another grammar point (e.g., passive voice).

____ A student asks for an explanation of something that I think is an exception or "just English," and I don't have a response.

____ A student asks a question about, say, a grammar point or punctuation rule. I don't recall the correct response and need some time to look it up.

____ A student asks, "Is this going to be on the test?"

____ A student asks a question that is completely unrelated to the lesson, such as, "When does the bookstore close?"

____ A student asks a question that I just answered.

10. Please comment on just one of the scenarios above. Choose one that you checked and tell <u>why it is problematic</u>, or one that you did not check and tell why you <u>don't view it as a problem</u>.

```
                                                              
                                                              
```

PART TWO: Planning Lessons

11. Do you write out a plan for every class session?

___ always
___ most of the time
___ sometimes
___ never

Comment?

```
                                                              
```

A typical lesson plan format that is taught to new teachers appears below.

```
LESSON PLAN:
    1. Warm up/review, or hook/motivation
    2. Explanation or presentation of new material
    3. Controlled practice with a focus on accuracy
    4. Communicative or open-ended practice
    5. Application/evaluation
```

12. Do you use this format or something similar?
___ always
___ most of the time
___ sometimes
___ never

13. Do you have a comment about the usefulness, strengths, or limitations of such a format for planning lessons? If so, please comment in the box.

[ ]

14. Whether or not you follow a format or write down plans, you probably keep some principles in mind as you plan your classes. Could you describe one or more of those?

[ ]

15. When planning your lessons, how do you allow for students who work at different paces?

[ ]

16. Many ESL teachers like to bring a variety of activities or games to their classrooms. Some examples of those might be "Find Someone Who," information gap, or reader's theater. The following questions ask about activities and games in your classroom.

17. Given the fact that activities and games take time for students to learn, how often do you introduce a *new* kind of activity in your class?
___ every class session
___ every week or two
___ a few times a semester
___ I don't use anything beyond what is in my textbook.

18. If you teach your class how to do an activity or play a game, do you generally repeat that activity or game with the same class?
___ No, once is enough.
___ I usually use the same activity/game a few times.
___ I repeat the same activity/game many times once the group is comfortable with it.
___ NA

Comments?

PART THREE: Pairs and Groups

19. On average, how often do your students work in pairs or small groups?
___ multiple times in each class session
___ once every class session
___ once every two or three class sessions
___ a few times a semester
___ never
___ other (please explain)

20. How do you form pairs or groups? Check all that apply.
___ let students work with their neighbors
___ pair weak with strong students
___ move students into ability groups (strong-strong, weak-weak)
___ mix native languages
___ put talkative students with quiet ones
___ create random groups
___ other (please explain)

21. Do you tend to pair or group students for a single class or part of a class, or do you use the same pairs or groups over several class meetings or several weeks?

___ short-term groups
___ long-term groups

22. If you have a preference for one over the other, please explain:

23. What do your students typically do when they work in pairs or small groups? Please check all that apply:

___ check homework exercises
___ do textbook exercises or other collaborative work
___ complete information gap activities
___ read aloud to each other
___ quiz each other
___ drill each other
___ have a conversation or discussion; interview each other
___ do research
___ plan or rehearse presentations; rehearse a dialogue or reader's theater
___ do collaborative writing (sentences, composition, dialogue, story)
___ peer review each other's writing
___ check each other's homework or quiz (swap papers)
___ other (please list or explain in the box)

24. In your experience, have you seen that some students are reluctant to work in pairs or groups? If so, what makes those students reluctant to work with others?

25. And what do you say to those students to convince them to work in pairs or groups?

[ ]

PART FOUR: Managing the Classroom Space

26. While explaining something to your class or introducing a new concept, where are you most frequently situated in the room? You may check all that apply.

___ sitting behind the teacher's desk
___ standing behind the teacher's desk or a podium
___ standing in front of or beside the teacher's desk
___ sitting on the teacher's desk
___ standing at the board or screen
___ standing behind a computer or other device such as a document camera
___ walking around

27. Why are you generally in one of the places you selected?

[ ]

28. While leading a whole-class discussion, where are you most frequently situated in the room? Please check all that apply.

___ sitting behind the teacher's desk
___ standing behind the teacher's desk or a podium
___ standing in front of or beside the teacher's desk
___ sitting on the teacher's desk
___ standing at the board
___ standing behind a computer or other device such as a document camera
___ walking around

29. Why are you generally in one of the places you selected?

[ ]

30. Where are you situated when your students are working in pairs or small groups? Please check all that apply.

___ I walk from group to group.
___ I sit down with each group for a while.
___ I stay in one part of the room, usually at the teacher's desk, to encourage students to work independently and figure things out on their own.
___ I stay at the teacher's desk and use the time to plan or grade papers.
___ I stay in one part of the room, by a computer, the board, or the teacher's desk, prepping the next part of the lesson.
___ I use the time to leave the room to make copies or run errands.

31. Comment on any of the above, or additional scenarios from your experience.

[ ]

32. How often are your students (all or some) out of their seats in your classes?

___ multiple times in each class session
___ once every class session
___ once every two or three class sessions
___ a few times a semester
___ never

Comment?

[ ]

33. For what reasons are your students out of their seats? Check all that apply

___ to write on the board
___ to find a partner or form a group
___ to participate in an activity like "Find Someone Who"
___ to present material to classmates
___ to play games
___ other (please explain)

PART FIVE: Classroom Trouble Spots

34. Which of the following would you consider to be the biggest disruption in your class?

___ Students arrive late.
___ Students take unauthorized breaks.
___ Students chat with each other.
___ Cell phones ring in class.
___ Students use phones to text or access the Internet.

35. What is your preferred approach in handling the disruption you indicated?

36. How do you minimize cheating on tests and quizzes?

37. Do you allow students to photograph notes that are written on your board or PowerPoint slides with their smart phones or tablets?

___ yes
___ no

38. Do you allow students to record your explanations?
___ yes
___ no

39. Please share any comments on student use of such technology in your classes.

[ ]

PART SIX: Lessons Learned

Check the extent to which you agree/disagree with the following. A box is provided beneath each for a comment.

40. I find it hard to strike the right balance between being approachable and friendly, and being respected as an authority in the room.

strongly agree   agree   neither agree nor disagree   disagree   strongly disagree

[ ]

41. I may be in control of the exercises and activities that students do in my class, but I am not in control of what they learn.

strongly agree   agree   neither agree nor disagree   disagree   strongly disagree

[ ]

42. Sometimes students just go through the motions and are not really engaged in learning.

strongly agree   agree   neither agree nor disagree   disagree   strongly disagree

[ ]

43. It's a good idea to bring jokes and humor into the classroom.

strongly agree   agree   neither agree nor disagree   disagree   strongly disagree

44. Classes sometimes "click" and sometimes don't, in spite of what I do as the teacher.

strongly agree   agree   neither agree nor disagree   disagree   strongly disagree

45. My teaching has been molded by my experience(s) learning a second or third language.

strongly agree   agree   neither agree nor disagree   disagree   strongly disagree

Appendix 3: Additional Data

In this Appendix, you will find complete responses to several of the questions in the survey when the figures included in the chapters had incomplete data. In one case (Question 45), there is no corresponding chart in the chapters.

From Figure 2, page 16

Q5. How do you communicate class rules to students?	
I provide students with a syllabus on the first day that outlines my class rules and policies.	65%
I provide a syllabus with some basic information, and then students brainstorm rules.	5%
I institute rules as the class progresses, and I learn more about their habits and personalities.	4%
I don't have any special rules in my class.	0%
Other	26%

From Figure 6, page 50

Q17. Given the fact that activities and games take time for students to learn, how often do you introduce a new kind of activity in your class?	
Every class session	1%
Every week or two	33%
A few times a semester	65%
I don't use anything beyond what is in my textbook.	1%

Appendix 3 199

From Figure 8, page 56

Q9. In a student-centered classroom, students should feel free to ask questions. This, however, can be problematic. Which of the follow do you see as disturbing the flow of your class?	
One student asks too many questions.	72%
A student asks a question that is completely unrelated to the lesson, such as, "When does the bookstore close?"	71%
A student asks a question that I just answered.	48%
A student asks, "Is this going to be on the test?"	26%
If I'm explaining a grammar point (e.g., present perfect), a student asks about another grammar point, (e.g., passive voice).	13%
A student asks a question about, say, a grammar point or punctuation rule. I don't recall the correct response and need some time to look it up.	6%
A student asks for an explanation of something that I think is an exception or "just English," and I don't have a response.	3%
If the class is working on grammar exercises, a student asks about the meaning of a word.	0%

From Figure 9, page 74

Q19. On average, how often do your students work in pairs or small groups?	
Multiple times in each class session	36%
Once in every class session	40%
Once every two or three class sessions	11%
A few times a semester	1%
Never	0%
Other	12%

From Figure 12, page 82, and Figure 13, page 93

Q23. What do your students typically do when they work in pairs or small groups? Please check all that apply.	
Have a conversation or discussion; interview each other	94%
Do textbook exercises or other collaborative work	88%
Plan or rehearse presentations; rehearse a dialogue or reader's theater	69%
Do collaborative writing (sentences, composition, dialogue, story)	67%
Peer review each other's writing	64%
Check homework exercises	57%
Complete information gap activities	49%
Do research	46%
Check each other's homework or quiz (swap papers)	68%
Quiz each other	37%
Read aloud to each other	31%
Drill each other	27%
Other	14%

From Figure 15, page 113

Q30. Where are you situated when your students are working in pairs or small groups? Please check all that apply.	
I walk from group to group.	96%
I sit down with each group for a while.	66%
I stay in one part of the room, usually at the teacher's desk, to encourage students to work independently and figure things out on their own.	44%
I stay in one part of the room, by a computer, the board, or the teacher's desk, preparing the next part of the lesson.	20%
I stay at the teacher's desk and use the time to grade papers.	10%
I use the time to leave the room and make copies or run errands.	5%

From Figure 16, page 123

Q32. How often are your students (all or some) out of their seats in your classes?	
Multiple times in each class session	29%
Once in every class session	44%
Once every two or three class sessions	18%
A few times a semester	10%
Never	0%

From Figure 17, page 124

Q33. For what reasons are your students out of their seats? Check all that apply.	
To find a partner or form a group	91%
To write on the board	85%
To present material to classmates	70%
To participate in an activity like Find Someone Who	49%
To play games	44%
Other	9%

This information is not previously presented.

Q45. My teaching has been molded by my experience(s) learning a second or third language.	
Strongly Agree	19%
Agree	52%
Neither Agree nor Disagree	15%
Disagree	10%
Strongly Disagree	5%

Index

Activities: in classrooms, 49–52; collaborative, 4, 92–93; icebreaker, 5–9; information gap, 94–95, 113; games, 50–52; low-risk, 92–93; new, 49–52; pair, 73–79

Answers, checking, in pair and group work, 88–90

Anticipation guides, 45, 83–84; versus open-ended discussion, 84–85

Assessment: as basis of teaching, 31–32; and lesson plans, 31–32, 45–46

Attendance, 14, 36. *See also* Late-arrivals/ Late-comers

Bingo, 49

Blackboard, use of in direct instruction, 106–107

Blended learning, 38

Bloom's taxonomy, 38

Boggle (game), 49, 165

Brainstorming, 7–8, 40, 46, 80, 118, 121, 160; think-pair-share in, 96; in whole-class discussion, 133

Breaks, taking unauthorized, 14, 151–152; movement of students and, 128–129

Case study problems, solving, 17

Cell phones: and cheating, 159; excluding, 15; ringing of, in class, 15, 162–163; taking photographs with, 167–168; texting on, 163–164; as tools, 164–170

Charades, 49

Chatting with other students, 153–161

Cheating: cell phones and, 159; versus helping, 154–160; preventing, on quizzes and tests, 174; preventing on quizzes and tests, 155–158; question-asker and, 157; view of, in U.S. culture, 160; writing compositions on, 160

Churchill, Winston, 63

Class discussion, use of textbook exercises for, 82–86; whole class, 130–132

Classes: allowing students to record, 175; disruptions, 145–146; giving quizzes at beginning of, 149–150; late arrivals to, 145–151; recording, 166–167, 175

Classroom. *See also* ESL classrooms; Student-centered classrooms: activities and games in, 49–52; tone in setting, 5–12; icebreakers in, 5–9; learning names in, 9–12

Classroom environment, 4–26; class rules in, 14–26; tone in, 5–12

Classroom interactions, 102–143

Classrooms: games in, 48–52, 94–95

Classroom trouble spots: arrivals and breaks, 144–175; chatting with neighbors, 153–154; helping versus cheating, 154–161, 174; recording of class, 175; smart phones, 162–171

Class rules, 14–26; amending, 18; for arriving late to class, 149–151; communication of by teachers, 16–18; English-only policies in, 18–22, 26; explaining to late arrivals, 146; Golden rule in, 14–16; for joining class late, 145–149; showing respect and, 145; for unauthorized breaks, 15–152

Class time, efficient use of, 43

Clicking of teachers with students in class, 183–185

Collaboration, 101, 118, 122, 125, 153–154, 161, 179; low-risk activities in, 92–93; in pair and group work, 87–88, 90–91

Communication. *See also* Oral communication: game-like, 94–95; oral, in bring variety to lesson plans, 43; student-to-student during, 157

Communicative approach, 71; paradigm shift from audiolingual method to, 82–83

203

Concentration (game), 49
Controversial topics: exercising caution with, 143; in fostering critical thinking, 142; scaffolding, in whole-class discussions, 135–139; in whole-class discussion, 134–135
Cooperative learning, 120
Critical thinking, 42; controversial topics in fostering, 142
Crossword puzzles, 49

Desks, arrangement of, in whole-class discussion, 131–132
Dictionaries: as app on smart phones, 165; avoiding use of, 15
Direct instruction; blackboard/whiteboard use in, 106–107; combining scaffolding and modeling with think-alouds, 109–111; teacher questions in, 107–109; teacher's place in room during, 103–106
Discussion. *See* Class discussion and Classroom interactions

English-only policies in class rules, 18–22

Fairness, use of L1s and, 22
Feedback, 45–46
Find Someone Who activity, 7, 49, 50, 126
First day, sensitivity on the, 25
First language: as issue in pair and group work, 75; use of, in classroom, 18–22, 26
Flipped ESL classrooms, 37–41, 103,

Games in classrooms, 49–52, 94–95
Goals, in lesson planning, 68
Golden Rule, 14–16
Grading: on a curve, 160
Grammar explanation: interruptions of, with questions, 58–59
Graphic organizers, 85
Group work, 4, 21, 27, 47–48, 67, 151, 184; as safe haven, 95–96 ; forming, 73–79; managing, 112–117; participation in, 117–122; short-term vs. long-term, 79–81, 100; student preferences in terms of groups, 100–101, 141. *See also* Pair and group work

Hangman (game), 49
Helping versus cheating, 154–161
Higher-order thinking, 41
Homework: assigning, 39–40; checking, in pair and group work, 90; copying classmates, 15–16 ; copying of, 160; pacing and, 48; reading aloud when checking, 92–93; time spent working on, 18
Humor, 57, 155–157, 181–183
Hybrid classes, 38. *See also* Flipped ESL classes

Icebreakers, 5–9, 122; Find Someone Who activity as, 6–7, 48, 50; late arrivals and, 146, 148; Two Truths and a Lie as, 7, 48, 50
Information gap activities, 94–95, 113
Interviews: structured pair, 6–7, 8, 90, 96; of teacher, 96
iPads, 96

Jeopardy (game), 49

Language. *See* First language; Second language
Late- arrivals/late-comers, for class, 145–151; planning for, 173–174
Learner-centered classroom. *See* Student-centered classrooms
Learning: blended, 38; cooperative, 120; task-based, 36–39
Lesson plans, 27–70; activities and games in, 49–52; assessment in driving, 31–32, 45–46; chunks in lesson plans, 43; flexibility in writing, 31; flipped, 36, 37–41; format for, 67; goals in, 68; guiding principles in, 42–46; need for variety in, 45; pacing in, 46–49; scaffolding in, 46; templates for, 33–37, 63–64; variety in, 42–54; whether teachers write out in advance, 28–33
Linguistic accuracy, 81–102
Listening, 42–43; asking questions and, 62; importance of, 12–13; pre-listening, 94
Low-risk collaborative activities, 92–93

Modeling, 109–110
Movement of teachers: building, into lesson plans, 123; of students around the room, 122–129; of students on class breaks, 128
Multiple choice tests, cheating on, 156, 157

Names: encouraging students to use each others', 11–12; teachers learning, 9–12, 25; tags, 10
Negative behaviors, addressing, 170–171
Note-taking (of students), 41, 133, 158, 166–169, 173, 175

Off-topic questions, 59, 60
Open-ended discussion: versus anticipation guides, 84; reasons for avoiding, 85–86
Oral communication. *See also* Communication: use of pair and group work in, 73
Over-planning, 29–30, 32

Pacing, in lesson planning, 43–44, 46–49
Pair and group work, 71–101; ability in, 78; avoiding long-term groups, 100; benefits of, 71–72; checking answers in, 88–90; checking homework in, 90; collaboration in, 87–88, 90–91, 122; completing and checking textbook exercises in, 86–91; cooperative learning in, 120; ensuring participation in, 117–122; formation of pairs and groups, 73–80; frequency of by teachers, 73–74; game-like communicative activities in, 94–95; how teachers form, 74–79; information gap activities in, 94–95, 113; integrating, with textbook exercises, 82–91; learning goals in, 112–113; low-risk collaborative activities in, 92–93; managing, 112–117; mixed abilities in, 77–79; overcoming reluctance in, 100–101; pacing in, 98; peer teaching and, 74–76; personality types in, 77–79; pitfalls in working with neighbors, 74; purpose of, 82–83; randomness in, 77, 79; reluctance of students, 100–101; role-plays in, 119–120; short-term versus long-term, 79–81, 100; in student-centered classroom, 97–98; turn-taking in, 121–122; types of tasks, 92–93; in writing classes, 96–98
Peer review, 49, 76–77, 80, 97
Peer teaching, 72, 74–75, 90, 154
Photographs, taking, with smart phones, 168, 193, 194
Pre-reading exercises, 83, 84
Presentations, 96, 109–110

Questions, 55–70; about grammar points, 58; articulation of, 61; balancing, 69–70; concerns about test, 59; disturbing the flow, 55–60; encouraging, 60–63; fear of asking, 60; off-topic, 59, 60; planning time for, 61; on previously covered material, 59, 60; request for further explanation or repetition, 62; on tests, 59; too many by students, 55–60, 69
Quizzes. *See also* Tests: creating alternate forms of, 156; giving, at beginning of class, 150; multiple choice, 156; open-ended, 156–157; preventing cheating on, 155–158, 175; true/false, 156

Read aloud, checking of homework exercises and, 92–93
Reader's theater, 96
Recording of classes, 165–167, 175
Role-plays, 95–96, 119–120
Rubrics, 46
Rules and policies. *See* Class rules.

Scaffolding, 46; combining with think-alouds, 109–111; of controversial topics, 135–138
Scrabble (game), 49
Smart phones. *See* Cell phones
Student(s): allowing to record classes, 175; arriving late, 145–151; 173–174; engaged in learning, 180–181; movement around the room, 122–129; movement in class break, 128; out of seats in class, 122–129, 141; preferences regarding groups, 141; standing by, in pair and group work, 122–129

Student-centered classrooms: active participation in, 12; asking questions in, 55–70; chatting to help in, 154; class rules in, 12–26; collaborative activities in, 4; guiding of flow in, 63; learners in, 4; lesson planning in, 27–70, 63–64; pair and group work in, 71–101; questions in, 70; students' presence in, 152; teachers in, 4, 22; whole-class discussions in, 130–132

Student interactions, 112–129; ensuring group participation, 117–122; managing group work and, 112–117; student movement around the room, 122–129

Syllabus, 17, 31

Task-based learning, moving toward, 36

Teachable moments, 31

Teachers: as authority figure, 176–178; and balance regarding planning in classroom, 66; burnout of, 32; in control of learning, 178–179; and controversial topics, 134–139; place in the room, 103–106, 130–132; moving around the classroom, 122–129; stand on L1 use, 18–22, 26; their L2 experiences, 52–54, 68–69; use of, as title, 170

Templates for lesson planning, 33–37, 64

Tests. *See also* Quizzes: concern over questions on, 58; preventing cheating on, 175; student-to-student communication during, 157

Textbook exercises: completing and checking, in pairs and groups, 86–91; integrating pair and group work with, 82–91; use of, for class discussion, 82–86

Texting, 163–164

Think-alouds, combining modeling and scaffolding with, 109–111

Thinking: critical, 42, 142; higher-order, 41

Think-pair-share strategy, 8, 44; in brainstorming, 96

Tone, setting in the classroom, 5–13; icebreakers in, 5–10

Tools, smart phones as, 164–170

Twenty Questions (activity), 49, 50; in pair-group work, 125–126

Two Truths and a Lie (activity), 7, 49, 50

Whiteboard use in direct instruction, 106–107

Who Am I? (game), 49; in yes-no questions, 125–126

whole-class discussion, 130–132; body language in, 132; controversial topics in, 134–139; recording ideas in, 132–134

Writing, 43; controversial topics in, 138; flexibility in, 31; need for quiet time for, 44; pair and group work in, 96–98; summaries, 110

Yes-no questions: in pair-group work, 125–127